T0305304

Beyond the Successful Veterinary Practice

OTHER IOWA STATE UNIVERSITY PRESS BOOKS BY THOMAS CATANZARO

Building the Successful Veterinary Practice

> *Volume 1* • *Leadership Tools*
> *Volume 2* • *Programs & Procedures*
> *Volume 3* • *Innovation & Creativity*

Veterinary Management in Transition:
Preparing for the Twenty-first Century

Beyond the Successful Veterinary Practice

Succession Planning & Other Legal Issues

Thomas E. Catanzaro, DVM, MHA, FACHE

Robert W. Deegan, DVM

Edward J. Guiducci, JD

Iowa State University Press / Ames

Thomas E. Catanzaro, DVM, MHA, FACHE, diplomate, American College of Healthcare Executives, received his DVM from Colorado State University, and his master's in healthcare from Baylor University. He is the only veterinarian to have achieved board certification in healthcare administration. Currently president and CEO of Catanzaro & Associates, a veterinary management consulting firm, Catanzaro is in wide demand as a consultant and speaker.

Robert W. Deegan, DVM, is the vice president for research and development at the Iowa JARD Corporation in Maquoketa, Iowa, which investigates agriculture options and develops commercial projects. He has worked with Catanzaro & Associates since 1993 to establish valuation methodology to evaluate fair market values for practices.

Edward J. Guiducci, JD, represents veterinarians in business and real estate transactions throughout the United States.

© 2000 Iowa State University Press
All rights reserved

Iowa State University Press
2121 South State Avenue, Ames, Iowa 50014

Orders:	1-800-862-6657
Office:	1-515-292-0140
Fax:	1-515-292-3348
Web site:	www.isupress.edu

Authorization to photocopy items for internal or personal use, or the internal or personal use of specific clients, is granted by Iowa State University Press, provided that the base fee of $.10 per copy is paid directly to the Copyright Clearance Center, 222 Rosewood Drive, Danvers, MA 01923. For those organizations that have been granted a photocopy license by CCC, a separate system of payments has been arranged. The fee code for users of the Transactional Reporting Service is 0-8138-1209-7/2000 $.10.

First edition, 2000

Library of Congress Cataloging-in-Publication Data

Catanzaro, Thomas E.
    Beyond the successful veterinary practice: succession planning & other legal issues/
Thomas E. Catanzaro, Robert W. Deegan, Edward J. Guiducci—1st ed.
        p.   cm.
    Includes bibliographical references (p.)
    ISBN 0-8138-1209-7
    1. Sale of small businesses—Planning. 2. Veterinary medicine—Practice.   I. Deegan, Robert W. II. Guiducci, Edward J.   III. Title.

SF756.4.C36 2000
636.089'068—dc21   00-039679

The last digit is the print number: 9 8 7 6 5 4 3 2 1

Contents

Preface

This publication is a general discussion of the subject matter and is intended to enhance the understanding of the readers. The publication is not intended to take the place of professional legal, accounting, or tax advice involving the readers' specific circumstances. Further, the readers should not utilize the examples of contracts contained within this publication without first consulting with professional advisers to obtain a thorough and proper understanding of the legal and tax effects. This is what Ed calls "legal disclosure and notice."

This publication is filling a void in our profession and, as such, has been a cooperative effort of Ed, Rob, and myself, as well as a reference text response to our clients and colleagues who have repeatedly requested this type of reference text. It also provides new graduates and new buyers the guidelines needed to negotiate their futures.

The accounting expertise in the veterinary profession is vested in a few noteworthy individuals like Owen McCafferty, Marsha Heinke, Cynthia Wychett, Lou Gatto, and some corporate consolidators. The legal expertise has less recognition since many with "JD" have never passed the bar or been accountable to the court, but that does not lessen their opinions or impact. This text is a response to the veterinarian's needs, not the attorney or accountant perspective of forensic medicine or liability reaction. It is a primer to allow the reader the ability to ask the right questions of local practice advisers.

Thomas E. Catanzaro, DVM, MHA, FACHE
Diplomate, American College of Healthcare Executives

Introduction

There are those who wondered after the leadership-based management trilogy, *"Building the Successful Veterinary Practice,"* published by Iowa State University Press (ISUP) in 1997 and 1998, *"What else is there to write?"* There are others who want to know all there is about succession planning and have not read the basic trilogy. And then there are those who ask, *"What the heck is succession planning?"* and *"Why do I need to take a leadership role just to sell my practice?"*

The answers are both easy and hard, and they are mostly practice-specific. Regardless, here are a few common threads of logic and operational concern:

- The one-doctor practice usually does not need a succession plan; the owner just sells the practice to the first veterinarian who is willing to pay close to the perceived selling price. The reciprocal is true; many one-doctor practices close without anyone being available to buy them, thereby losing all inherent value.

- Most veterinary practices have grown to 2.6 veterinarians or more during the last decade of the 20th century. This makes the perceived selling price "out of range" for most lone veterinarians who want to "buy a practice."

- Practices are selling from as low as tangible assets (these are the "no net" practices) to about 80 percent of the annual three-year-averaged gross (these are the practices that have a 9-15 percent net, after doctor compensation and reasonable ROI deductions). When the practice is producing over 15 percent net, after ALL doctor compensation and reasonable ROI deductions, the seller can often get over 80 percent of the annual three-year-averaged gross. Regardless, no practice is worth any more than what someone is willing to pay for it.

- Medical record sufficiency, client return rates, community demographics, and a host of other influences affect the selling price, and most accountants do not know how to value a practice using these factors. This text attempts to clarify some of these critical factors, but the number-crunching accountants will seldom understand this practice-philosophy-based logic.

• When selling a practice, the veterinary practice healthcare delivery team, which can offer a continuity of care with bonded clients, can increase the value of the practice entity to the buyer, mainly by keeping the clients returning until they can re-bond with the new practitioner(s).

The review of the ISUP trilogy *Building the Successful Veterinary Practice* would not be simple enough to fit into this introduction, but some very important practice and community leadership relationships can be graphically illustrated.

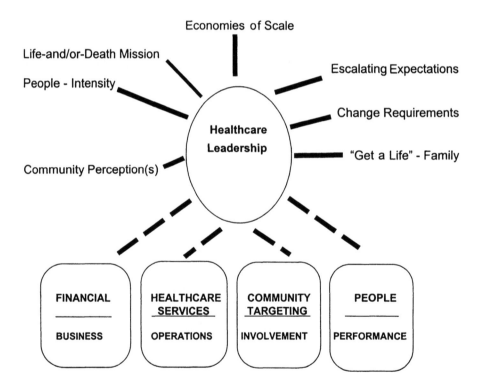

The healthcare 2000 confluence diagram reflects the dynamics of the new millennium; it will confuse the traditionalists. Looking at examples of some of the elements illustrates why:

Economies of Scale. Internal practice referrals to another doctor or nurse on staff, affiliations with specialists and emergency practices, or even just simple buying corporations

Escalating Expectations. The client who comes in with an Internet printout, second generation pet owners who want higher quality care, or even increased client access hours

Life-and/or-Death Mission. The "urgent care" case, nasal oxygen, or new diagnostic accuracy

People Intensity. Client demands, staff demands, and even new associate doctor demands

Change Requirements. Faster service, pet health insurance, or even personal financial planning

Community Perception. James Herriot, Animal Planet, and even community leadership

Get a Life. Balanced lifestyle, outside interests, ample vacation/benefits for all.

The four boxes at the bottom must provide a balanced foundation for a practice ownership to be fiscally viable for succession planning.

When addressing the succession planning needs of any practice, the ability to assess the outside influences (opportunities and threats) is just as critical as the ability to develop the inside influences (strengths and weaknesses). All of these factors come together at the leadership position of the practice. Yet many practice owners want to be involved in the moment-to-moment operations, thereby condemning themselves to a life of enslavement (a hard life to "sell" to another doctor). The only way for a practice owner to survive this confluence of dynamic pressures is to develop a team that can keep the practice flow in perspective.

When developing the veterinary practice group, there are leadership skills which can be used (Appendix B, Volume 1, *Building the Successful Veterinary Practice: Leadership Tools,* published by Iowa State University Press (ISUP) in 1998, reflects the 14 critical skills) to move the team through FORMING and STORMING to NORMING and PERFORMING. Volume 1 discusses when to use the various leadership styles: Directing, Persuading, Coaching, Delegating, Consulting, and Joining (from authoritative to democratic, all are needed at some time during a healthcare delivery day). The difference often lies in the team that is developed and the fact that the team players can be grouped into three groups [as opposed to the four D-I-S-C behavior categories (*Dominant—Inspirational—Steady—Conscientious*) that practice environments can cause]. The groupings are summarized in the following.

~~ ORGANIZATIONAL GROUP DYNAMICS ~~

GROUP COMPOSITION	PERCENT OF ORGANIZATION	FEAR DYNAMICS
SUPERSTARS	15-20%	
☆ Outstanding Self-Motivation		☹ Excellence Opportunities
☆ Thrive on Challenges		☹ Regression
☆ Define the System(s)		☹ Competitive Edge
STEADY/STRONG PLAYERS	60-70%	
☆ Steady Performance		☹ Job Security
☆ Strive To Succeed		☹ Job Stability
☆ Support the System(s)		☹ Future Focus
NON-PLAYERS	10-15%	
☆ Questionable Performance		☹ Workload
☆ Self-Centered		☹ New Tasks
☆ Eradicate the System(s)		☹ Job Expansion

The superstars are special resources, often overcommitted by ownership because they will do so much, so well, without constant supervision. The steady and strong players need some special attention, usually on a daily basis with your morning coffee, by visiting them on-station and sharing basic comments like *"What can I do to help you make things better?,"* or *"I really liked how you handled _____ yesterday,"* or even, *"I would like to address _____. Can you think of any way we could make it better?"* For both superstars and the steady/strong team members, please remember the 3Rs of good staff relations: RESPECT, RESPONSIBILITY, RECOGNITION!

Sometimes the non-players are the tenured team members within the practice, and sometimes they are "bought with the practice" and evolve (by definition, those who evolve will no longer be "non-players"). During the organizational renewal of the practice systems, the non-players will use terms like:

- If it ain't broke ... we don't need to fix it!
- We tried that before but ... it will never work!
- It is not in my ... job description!
- We have always ... done it that way!
- We can't do that because ... we are understaffed!

Walk, don't run, when addressing these "non-players"; they should be assessed using a systematic method for effective transition. They are in need of compassionate dehiring, not just uncaring firing. They have been with the practice for a reason, and many have client bonds that will have to be transferred to the new team members. So in the dehiring process, have a plan for transferring clients from the non-players to the strong players. Don't overload the superstars on the practice team; they will load themselves as the need becomes evident, before you even know what is happening. To make things better for all the players, establish HOUSE RULES early in the development cycle. These are especially important at staff meetings and when causing the non-players to decide to move on to another job. The basic house rules may vary from practice to practice, but the following are often used as starting points:

SAMPLE HOUSE RULES
✓ Internal issues stay backstage!
✓ Anytime is a good time to get assistance.
✓ Be prepared to discuss solutions to problems—not just frustrations!
✓ If you cannot see the caring intentions of another, do not start the debate.
✓ Everyone is an emissary to our clients all the time!

Regardless of your skill as a leader, mistakes will happen. Some things won't work because the moon or stars are wrong, sometimes the client flow is atypical, or in some cases, the training is inadequate (actually, the latter is most common). But one thing is for sure: if you ever decide to blame someone or something, you have abdicated accountability for the resolution. You cannot blame anyone or anything if you want to review mistakes; you must address the real issues confronting the practice and team.

MISTAKE REVIEW MATRIX
✓ Here is WHAT happened!
✓ Here is Why it happened!
✓ From this, I learned _____— and we learned _____.
✓ Next time, I'll do _____—and we will do _____.

When evaluating the "next change step" in any program or procedure, the approach must be pro-active . . . the chaos of change is controlled only by making change a regular practice process. Continuous quality improvement (CQI) has four input elements:

Practical + Pertinent + Patient-focused + Progressive = Pay-Off!

What is the best pay-off you can imagine? If you quickly say "money," you have missed the target. In Volume 2, *Building the Successful Veterinary Practice: Programs & Procedures,* published by Iowa State University Press (ISUP) in 1998, we shared an expanded chart of accounts, budgets, and compensation programs, but we also shared client bonding concerns and improved practice image ideas, pro-active internal promotions, continuity of care with better medical records, and performance planning. These are the elements that come together to form a better practice, as shown in the "Healthcare 2000 Confluence Dynamics" diagram. But individually, no one element or current gimmick can make a difference that will hold for the long run during any succession plan or while the practice is evolving. The bottom line is making client satisfaction occur (exceeding their expectations), and that is summarized below:

C	"Core value" driven
L	Lead to the future
I	Innovation
E	Excellence
N	Neighborhood focus
T	Timely strategic response (SWOT)
$	Fiscal capability
★	Staff pride

So with all of this review, succession planning is not just for the owner; it is for the practice itself, as well as for every team member. Succession planning could be individual career planning, it could be the development of special practice services to meet community demands (demographics), or it could even be an ownership issue (mental or fiscal), but regardless, it is always for the long range, for the future. Succession planning is done by taking baby steps, as well as by using solid management and leadership principles and skills, which can be replicated by others as the foundation of the "practice renewal" effort and community-centered growth response.

Succession planning is evolutionary and necessary—it allows a practice's ownership to be addressed separately from healthcare delivery leadership. It is not the "strategic planning" of the last decade, but rather, a strategic response to react to community dynamics and emerging opportunities. This text opens the doors and windows of the "limited perspective" seen in most practices and practice advisers. It takes the reader "outside the box" while providing fiscal and legal insights to protect all the players.

Beyond the Successful Veterinary Practice

Succession Planning— Forces of Change

1

*All business proceeds on beliefs, or judgements, or
probabilities, and not on certainties.*
—Charles W. Eliot

Succession planning is the slow but deliberate process of altering the leadership structure of the practice to better prepare for tomorrow. The most significant challenge that faces our veterinary profession today is not competition nor recession, but rather, our own ability to change the habits that got us where we are today. This supports the old adage, "If you are satisfied with what you've done to get where you are, you will stagnate and die." The influx of corporate America into the veterinary profession reflects two emerging parameters: 1) there is money to be made, and 2) the traditional veterinary healthcare delivery systems (isolationism) of the 1970s and 1980s are not serving the needs of the community. One author, Robert B. Tucker, captured many of these concepts in his book, *Managing the Future* (ISBN 0-399-13576-6), and has categorized ten driving forces of change for the '90s, specifically, factors that influence the consumer's behavior. I have used Tucker's ten forces and Catanzaro & Associates' consulting experience to apply these driving forces to situations most practitioners encounter today.

Dynamics of Change

Tucker makes a great opening statement that bears remembering: "The best way to predict the future is to invent it!" In the recent Iowa State University Press leadership text, *Building the Successful Veterinary Practice: Innovation & Creativity*, Volume 3, we explored the learning organization and the creative process that leaders can instill.

The premise of change management is that you must first **create some form of dissatisfaction or discomfort**, centered around a specific habit (e.g., vaccine price sensitivity due to large format retailer "media blitz" efforts), rather than around life or the practice. Then you need to **find an alternative model**, something that anticipates the future needs of the practice (e.g., ten-minute, fast-in-fast-out, nurse-based, wellness vaccination appointments). The third step is to **develop the process of change**, the constant reinforcement of the new model in operation until it becomes habit (e.g., *Preferred Client* access to these "economic benefit" programs). In simpler terms, the process is as follows:

1. Unfreeze the old habit.
2. Reform the specific activity into a new shape or model.
3. Refreeze the new model into a habit.

If we look at the superstores offering pet healthcare, the veterinary public-owned complexes, or the affiliated practice markets, we see that economies of scale help them to some degree, but the real reason for their success is that they see veterinary medicine as a business and, as such, make business decisions on a regular basis. They are not going to go away, nor can an individual practitioner effectively "compete" with them on their playing fields. The secret to practice success is to define your *own* playing field, and the key to succession planning is to have a clear three- to five-year plan of leadership transition for the new millennium. Revolutionary (not evolutionary) success lies in making business decisions in your own practice and NOT WORRYING about the other practice. The three main reasons for this practice owner attitude are

1. As long as you "blame" someone or something else, you will never decide to cope with the realization that you must control your own environment. You must adapt to the changing community.
2. Positive thought begets positive action, while negative thought begets negative action. Healthcare must be carried out in a positive environment to succeed.
3. Every practice has areas where services may be enhanced, where programs may be expanded, or even areas where some process is continued because "it's always been that way." This is a sure sign of a need to change!

Now that you have developed the "quit worrying about other practices" attitude and have started to realize that as a leader you must make decisions to change, you can see why change is inevitable. The ten driving forces that make change in the business market inevitable and predictable, according to Tucker, are:

TUCKER'S TEN FORCES OF CHANGE
- *Speed*—exploiting the "FedEx" imperative
- *Convenience*—creating the "Domino" effect
- *Age Waves*—"Sleep Inns" demographic changes
- *Choice*—"Have it your way" Burger King marketing
- *Lifestyle*—changes of "McCormick" spices
- *Discounting*—"Help-U-Sell" real estate consulting fees
- *Value Added*—the "Four Seasons Hotels" customer profile
- *Customer Service*—the "Marriot" philosophy
- *Techno-Edge*—10,000 hand-held computers for Frito-Lay
- *Quality*—demonstrated by Rolex, Ford, Disney, etc.

To the informed reader, the companies and stories in Tucker's book offer insight, but to the novice, they provide only interesting stories. The *Bible* teaches us that teaching in parables is the most effective method to get the ideas across to the masses. The *One Minute Manager* made this style of management popular, and most of the current best sellers in management use this same technique (e.g., *Managing from the Heart*). As such, we will continue this trend as we explore practice situations in the ten areas of forces of change.

Veterinary Medical Applications for the Ten Forces of Change

- *Speed* has become the number one concern of most Americans, and becomes a practice opportunity when we look at our client needs. Some practices track the sign-in and wait times right on the circle sheet and offer premiums (e.g., free ice cream cone certificate) if practice delays cause extended waits. An emerging trend in communities where the Yellow Pages are full of "appointment only" and "appointment required" veterinary ads, the tag line, "WALK-INS WELCOMED," is good for a 25 percent increase in front door traffic. Certain practices, usually located in "bedroom" commuter communities, exploit the "day care" drop off service for established clients by having a technician available during commuter hours, regardless of the appointment hours. Some practices compete with the superstores not by simply offering competitive prices, but also by offering a "fast in-fast out," appointment-based, no waiting, specific wellness program to deliver the services or products to the consumer. *"People you know"* and *"no lines"* are strong advantages when differentiating your practice from a large format superstore.

- *Convenience* is an intangible factor that most veterinary clients understand, which is why 60 percent of the pet owners select their initial practice based on location. Compounding this location dependence is the fact that over 60 percent of American households are dual income or single parent, meaning the veterinary needs must be met on evenings or weekends unless time is taken off work. Companion animal practices that offer early morning drop-off services and evening or extended weekend hours are finding not only very grateful clients, but also clients who hadn't accessed them before due to inconvenience. The owners at a Georgia practice, in a metroplex bedroom community, exploited this need by changing their weekday appointment hours to noon to 8 p.m.; their business has increased weekly (and they concurrently reduced the required payroll hours).

- *Age Waves* is a fancy term for the "mature market" (growing five times faster than any other group), the "baby boomers," and the "baby bust" that followed. In Des Moines, our demographic report revealed a practice location that supported a community area with virtually no one between the ages of 30 and 45 (the prime pet owning ages), and the gross showed it. In Florida, we see more practices establishing a pet ambulance service for elderly shut-ins. In certain areas of the country, we find only part-time veterinarians are available; these are dedicated and competent graduates who don't want the practice ownership commitment. Some traditional-minded practices that want only full-time associates willing to work 60 to 80 hours a week, cannot find "suitable" veterinarians to employ, while other colleagues in the same community use flexible hours as a benefit of employment and get more opportunities for associates than they can handle.

- *Choice* for veterinary clients is not always a "yes" or "no" situation. A well-trained practice staff offers two "yes" options and gets a "yes" on a pre-qualification statement (e.g., *"Is this the level of care that you are looking for?"*). These procedures give the impression of "choices" while ensuring a sale closure. Some practices offer their comprehensive geriatric program ("baseline" ECG, laboratory profile, X-ray, and dental), but phase the diagnostics over weekly, monthly, or quarterly increments that better fit the budget and commitment of their clients. Smarter practices offer their geriatric program as a fall arthritis screening program (when the cool air causes lameness or at least slower responses), or a lead II screening ECG for murmur identification, or as an internal organ screening blood chemistry to establish a baseline for the "golden years." Some practices have opened a "cat annex" in close proximity to their practice for their feline clients who don't like the danger of facing dogs. These practices have pulled clients from other practices due to the exclusive care (and name) alone. Some practitioners even use client surveys to determine which choices are important to their clients and then promote those specific services in an outreach program.

- *Lifestyle* preferences have been ignored by many but capitalized on by a few. New ideas include "life cycle annual consultations," charging extra for "cat condos" and "boarding playtime," and promoting specialized care for caged mammals and birds. The initial California reaction was to expand retail and make veterinary practices "one-stop" shopping sites; then other practices in the USA tried to follow. Those retail areas are shrinking, however, when faced with the larger format retail superstores. Many clients enter a veterinary facility stressed and are not looking for a shopping experience; smart practices look for ways to decrease the stress, selling "peace of mind" rather than just pushing products and services. A few practices have catered to the single parent by establishing a children's play corner, or, as in the case of a Canadian practice we visited, a sunken area with play areas fenced into the window wells. All of these are examples of ways to improve your practice's environment to meet the changing needs of the community. You must decide which changes can improve the "feeling" of your practice.

- *Discounting* has spread into almost all businesses, but it has been used very ineffectively in veterinary medicine. "Loss leaders" do not work in healthcare unless there is a very large volume of available clients who float between practices. Healthcare has a trust and client-bonding feature that keeps quality clients from following the low-priced coupon. The strategy to lead rather than react has led some practices to offer a specific number of "subsidized pet population control surgeries" each week, or a "caring client rebate" for a nail trim done with bathing and grooming ($63 value for only $41). We at Catanzaro & Associates prefer to help our clients identify a profitable "2 for 1" deal (e.g., two parasite screening fecals for the price of one still has net), especially with cat owners, since the average cat household contains two or more cats. The "PREFERRED CLIENT" program discussed in Volume 3, *Building the Successful Veterinary Practice: Innovation & Creativity,* specifically addresses the "bring them back more often for more net" concept or preferred pricing for bonded, but cash-limited, clients. Some practices have found that just putting the words "NOW ONLY" in front of their vaccine, bath/dip, spay, or neuter price gives the perception of a discount without the associated loss of gross income. Practices that have offered a comprehensive wellness program (e.g., Health Maintenance Agreement (HMA), new puppy program, or new kitten program) have listed a prepayment savings with the annual fee ($245 value for only $135). The new National Pet Health Insurance Programs now offer $2 of reimbursable wellness coverage for every $1 of premium, yet many practices fail to "see the benefit" and continue to discount themselves into poverty.

- *Value Added* has been evident in the puppy/kitten vaccination programs, where prepayment allows the client to receive behavior management assistance (e.g., house training techniques with a nice refrigerator poster) for no additional cost. Some of the practices Catanzaro & Associates support have used a value-added concept of including "puppy clubs" or "kitten carrier classes" with the vaccination (e.g., two class tickets, each a $19.50 value, distributed with each vaccination); others have added value benefits to their heartworm treatment programs or other inpatient services. Whenever a traditional "no charge" service is priced but then rebated on the invoice, a value has been added in the client's perception. The smarter practices now send a value-added thank you premium to clients who refer new clients; no-strings attached premiums like two tickets to the movies, zoo, or local sporting events are far more impressive to the client than offering nominal healthcare discounts (and it is tax deductible advertising, unlike discounts which are absorbed).

- *Customer Service* can overcome moderate price advantages, but it must be a total philosophy. We speak for the needs of the pet and allow the client the right to say no; we then validate whatever decision the client makes. Most veterinary practices say they care, but then they under-staff the reception desk. Even worse, no one at the practice understands patient advocacy. In these practices, narratives have seldom been rehearsed or refined so the staff member is comfortable with the words and the outcome expectation. The cost of one extra employee is paid for by gaining or retaining one extra client a day. The more progressive practices, like one on the Gulf Coast of Mississippi, hire an "off-line telephone receptionist" concurrent with the second veterinarian to remove the distraction from the front desk. Most practices never check on a client's or patient's well-being when an appointment is missed (same day call) or call after ten days to see how a 21-day cystitis treatment is progressing. They will send a new client a thank-you letter but will seldom call between appointments to see if the client has questions. A few practices have exploited the Age Wave by using "greeters" (yes, just like at your local Wal-Mart) from the local retirement village who love to talk and make people feel welcome.

- *Techno-Edge* is beyond ultrasound and endoscopy, it means using the tools that allow you to communicate more quickly with specific target populations. A target mailing, such as a "Health Alert" to only multi-cat households, or to clients with dogs over five years old that have not had a kidney function profile established, makes marketing much more effective when the clients come in for services. Using 1990 census data to determine specific population preferences within areas of the community allows a tailored approach to new outreach programs. Using medical or surgical technology to "overcome" the historical odds (e.g., for geriatrics and isoflurane for birds) is another effective method of using "high tech" to promote practice "high touch" techniques. Some practices have even hooked up a video camera to the laboratory microscope so clients can see parasites (or eggs) on a monitor from the comfort of the examination room. The new 32-bit Windows software technology allows many diagnostic tools (hand-held veterinary scopes, otoscopes, ECGs, etc.) to be directly linked and recorded into the computer's data base medical record for visual descriptions to clients as well as for future change comparisons.

- *Quality* is the single greatest key in healthcare, or any other industry, for long-term profitability. The human healthcare field has promoted Continuous Quality Improvement (CQI) as its answer to total quality management (TQM) (as described by authors like W.
Edwards Deming and J.M. Juran). The basic premise of CQI is that
all healthcare workers MUST be empowered to improve their environment, or the client's encounter with the facility; the requirement
to make improvements or enhancements (changes) must be an accountability accepted by every member of the staff. The Joint Com-
mission for the Accreditation of Hospitals, IBM, Hertz, ITT Shera-
ton, Disney, and most every other major business organization have
determined that "quality" is a special edge. Specifically, a client perception must be seen as a business output of a veterinary practice,
while "pride" is the critical hospital staff business input. Raising the
client's knowledge of veterinary medical concerns is part of this
process, and, to that end, some practices have established focus
groups, "Client Councils" of a dozen clients, to advise them on matters of quality perceptions. (The same dozen is not always required
or even suggested.) One of the critical elements required for continuous quality improvement (CQI) is the accountability for success being vested in the staff, allowing them to make their jobs better every
day WITHOUT permission. This requires recurring staff training,
supplied by caring leadership in the learning organization. Some
practices have even made continuing education a requirement for
continued employment.

The Competitive Advantage

Understanding the forces that drive change as we enter the new millennium is not enough for success or succession planning. Telling your
staff to have pride in what they do does not meet the change need either. Failing to develop potential income dollars in an attempt to save
expense pennies is not the secret to success. The commitment to change
starts at the top; practices are led by example. The adage "What you
do speaks so loud that I can't hear what you are saying" must be remembered by every veterinarian and practice owner, whether working
within the hospital environment or participating in community activities. If the leader spends time blaming the events of the community
(e.g., publicly-owned veterinary practices, superstores, or networked
affiliated practices) as a reason for slow business, so will the staff. If

the practice leader follows the dairyman's lead, "Don't cry over spilt milk, just find another cow to milk," the solutions will come from within the team. If the team members are expected to find better ways to do things (CQI), they will if the leader consistently implements over 70 percent of the suggestions.

The easy days of veterinary practice growth are over; there are already colleagues offering alternatives to your clients. The good news from PetStuff® (before they were merged into PetsMart®) was that 45 percent of the clients who accessed them did not have a veterinarian; PetStuff® was actually expanding the client pie size. Another good aspect of PetStuff® was that they offered the local practices the opportunity to staff and operate PetStuff® veterinary wellness facilities IF the local practitioners referred the sick animals to their own hospitals and followed up on the clients seen at PetStuff® from their own hospitals. This was different from PetsMart® and VetSmart® and most other "wellness vendors," but it still offered a working model for alternative delivery modalities; it was a "change" in the basic tenets of practice. The driving forces of change are going to get more demanding; they will not disappear. Leading the changes in your practice and community marks the difference between success and failure. The importance of a long-term practice plan that embraces innovation, creativity, and flexibility has never been more important than it will be in the new millennium. The competitive advantage will be gained by those veterinary practices that learn to use the team approach to healthcare. By empowering staff members to individually pursue excellence within a clear set of practice goals and expectations, the strengths of many will be brought to bear on the forces of change.

Evolution of Succession Needs

The only thing certain about tomorrow is that you can't stop it from coming!

Twenty years ago, veterinary medicine averaged one doctor per practice, and it took a population of about 10,000 to support a full-time veterinarian. Now we have practices averaging 2.6 doctors and only a population of 4000 per full-time equivalent (FTE) veterinarian. Twenty years ago, the one-doctor practice had a value between $250,000 and $300,000. Now the 2.6-doctor practices have estimated values in the $800,000-plus range. At 20 percent down, the one-doctor practice was within the reach of most practitioners for purchase, but few professional individuals can raise the $150,000-plus down payment needed to procure a veterinary practice today. At Catanzaro & Associates, we now see a much greater need for practice owners to develop a succession plan for ownership, and we are called in more often to help with the transition.

Succession Examples

Dr. A.L. was the patriarch of his practice, supported quietly by his wife, who was a wonderful practice asset. He hired an associate and put her on a developmental program, and eventually she used her "minority status" to buy half with government money. The practice has grown to a 3.5-doctor practice (the patriarch is the half-time practitioner). Dr. A.L. had cardiac bypass surgery and needed his associate to assume more accountability for the practice; she was not ready and resisted. He resumed the role of patriarch, and a status quo emerged until the health of his wife and his own lack of energy forced the succession issue to re-emerge. Catanzaro & Associates had to build a system of support from within the staff to support the new owner, but she was not the decisive owner envisioned by the patriarch. Dr. A.L. still struggles to become comfortable enough with her style to let go of the practice operations.

Dr. P.R. had retired in place (RIP) but still operated his practice as a small one-doctor practice. The practice had experienced no growth, the annual gross had been $175,000 +/- $25,000 for the past four years, and the facility was not current. Dr. P.R. wanted to sell, but no one was interested in an outdated, one-exam room, no-surgery facility. We started with the facility, adding an inpatient expansion constructed at only 12 percent of what a "veterinary specific architect" estimated an expansion would cost. We then added an entry level, single station, veterinary computer system and upgraded the patient advocacy of the doctor. Within four months, he reached the point where $1000 days were the minimum, and he was routinely cresting to $2000-plus days during the busy seasons. He began having fun and feeling a sense of pride again and decided not to retire immediately. After three years, we were ready to market the practice but had to start from scratch since the *"associate we had added and developed over two years"* decided in the eleventh hour that she did not want to commit to the practice purchase.

Drs. R & A had a mixed animal practice, were married (to each other), and needed relief, so they brought another couple into the practice as associates. The relationship was solid, and eventually Drs. R & A sold a share of the practice to the new associates. Thus, two couples—four doctors—were owners of a solid four-doctor practice. As such, they had to hire an unneeded associate to allow each of the couples to take appropriate time off. The partnership agreement also called for a sabbatical arrangement. To take off long periods of time, however, the business operations had to be slowly transferred to the new ownership couple, something they did not really desire. Catanzaro & Associates had to build a system of operational management tracking that the new couple could monitor and manage while giving them a better cash flow to allow the hiring of an additional associate during the sabbatical (actually hired by the couple on sabbatical from their partnership monies).

Over his career, Dr. G.B. had built a successful three-facility complex, had established his retirement plan early, and had invested wisely in stocks, real estate, and other assets. His son had joined the practice, there were three other associates with over a decade of tenure each, and Dr. G.B. had a good handle on the programs and procedures which cause liquidity. When he got ready to retire, he simply gave the four doctors (son plus three) 24 percent of the practice each with the simple explanation that he had all the money he wanted, three homes, and had already educated his family. The problems occurred when the four doctors could not replicate what the one doctor had done. Their attempt at management was "number heavy" (comparing percentages) but without common sense or a program/procedure basis. We had to recalibrate the team and their approach, plus help them realize that each of the three practices were different entities. We also had to reintroduce the "program-based" budget system, which was common to the original owner's technique of leadership. (He did not call it "program-based budgeting," but his logic was client-centered and procedure-smart.)

Rules of Thumb

As a rule of thumb, I hate rules of thumb. Regardless, we need some guidelines to start these discussions. Some of the following rules of thumb are common sense, so take each with a grain of *NaCl*:

- The banks, Small Business Administration, and other lenders will NOT lend money on blue sky (goodwill, projected earnings, etc.) so

remember projected earning value must become the down payment
in most practice sale deals UNLESS you are willing to carry the paper.

- Your building and land should be in a separate "land and cattle
company" (LLC, family trust, or some other shelter), and you
NEED to be paying yourself a reasonable rent (e.g., 7-10 percent).
And yes, this saves federal taxes every month, as well as at the end
of the career, especially if the "real estate entity" is not within the
practice owner's estate.

- If the practice is solely owned, and has multiple associates, consider
a junior partner with your tenured professional team, a "stair-step"
purchase option that allows small shares to be systematically purchased by the favored doctor over a prolonged period of time.

- If the practice has many partners and few associates, ensure you
have some form of "first death" protection insurance. The ownership of the policy should belong to a legal entity other than yourself
(this keeps the proceeds out of the $600,000 estate tax), and the
beneficiary needs to be kept current (and again, it should not be the
practice entity for estate and taxation reasons).

- The old valuation system of taking the annualized average of three
years' gross as the practice price is valid ONLY if 1) the practice has
experienced 20 percent net growth annually, 2) there is no debt,
AND 3) someone is willing to buy the practice at that price (it is rare
to find this point combination in today's buyer market). The "70-80
percent of gross" rule of thumb is becoming more accurate for the
average companion animal practice. Specialty practices and food animal practices have a value in real assets but little else. Reputations
carry these practices, so some form of partnership or shared ownership is essential to increase their value at retirement.

- The practice sale preparation needs to start at least three years BE-
FORE the anticipated separation date since net must be increased
(every valuation formula is "net sensitive"). Actually, five years before the anticipated sale, smart sellers quit laundering money
through the practice (hiding expenses and salaries). Then, in the
fourth year, the sellers establish a growth and promotion plan that
will cause a growing practice profile over the next half-decade.

- The transition of ownership and practice leadership should be initiated a full business cycle before the anticipated retirement date since
the practice's leadership must be transferred smoothly for the purpose of staff and client retention. This often requires a mediator (a

qualified consultant and mentor) to assist all parties in maintaining harmony and practice pride (*quality is what the clients call pride*).

- If you are a young practitioner, start banking/investing 10 percent of your take-home every month, effective immediately, with NO excuses. Also, at the end of every year, whether you are a practice owner or a productivity-based associate getting an end-of-year bonus, place 50 percent of the excess net into solid real estate land investments in your own community. In this manner, practice sale becomes supplemental money, not primary retirement money.

These points are being made here simply because too many practices fail to plan ahead—and **the public veterinary corporations are NOT always the answer.** If you cannot see your practice days ending or you only see one method of exit, then succession planning is even more critical. Succession planning is how to move from one level of your veterinary medical evolution to the next level of your life. It needs to be done today and committed to completely, regardless of at what evolutionary level you are, since life and family are long-lasting, and practice is transitory. *Today is already yesterday's tomorrow,* and nothing stopped it from happening. Learn from that fact. Plan for the future and it won't be scary.

What's Your Practice Worth?

The usual way of looking at practice value is to estimate the sum of money an owner could get by selling the practice. This is best expressed as a sum of the assets and the return over expenses; although in reality, it is ONLY what someone is willing to pay for the practice. But contrary to the CPA versions of valuation (examples in Appendix A), the assets of the practice are much greater than the monetary price; the only thing all the assets have in common is that they need to be maintained regularly by people and be in a constant state of improvement by people for an in-depth, skill-based discussion of continuous quality improvement by well-led teams.

We all recognize that beyond the cash and equipment in a practice value, there are the human assets; beyond the human assets are the visions of the owners, leaders, and staff. The discussion of value becomes wider than just bookkeeping; vision is more than expense control; succession planning is sharing the plan, not just selling.

It's what you do with what you got that counts.
— Lesley Dunlap

One of the most under-utilized practice assets is the staff. Here, maintaining value means enlisting their brains and hearts as well as their bodies for practice enhancement. The staff members need to know "why" something is happening, especially if they are the ones who are expected to explain why it's important to clients. The staff is the first market for any program, and if they are not "sold" on the concept, they will not have pride in it. If the staff has no pride, the effort will never succeed. In succession planning, this means

- It is becoming far smarter to "grow your own" successor(s) than to try to sell the practice on the open market.
- Investing outside the practice, building independent retirement resources by small investments each month, and legally separating the building/land from the practice so "landlord money" can continue after the practice stops.
- It is essential to start "letting go" of the control that built your success when the practice approaches a two-doctor practice.
- Delegation to others requires 1) training to a level of trust, 2) persuasion of others that "they can do it," and 3) coaching to fine tune the skills and knowledge.

Paraprofessional and professional staff, as well as owners, need to be nurtured; **respect, responsibility** and **recognition** are the "key three" elements in the organization's environment. If we assume that those three elements exist in the practice environment, we must address another critical element of the top six staff satisfaction elements: a quality compensation program. If we are to "grow succession elements" from within, we must provide a liveable wage (with benefits) and retirement plan that makes people want to stay.

There are many ways that money can be considered the "root of all evil," but without it, nothing else can occur. In fact, without money, the front door gets locked by the bank and it can never swing again. The major problem in veterinary medicine is that we are a young profession, and, as such, we are defining the business as we go. The first companion animal hospital was built in 1929, and the American Animal Hospital Association was started in 1938; this means most practice owners learned from "some guy" (yes Jane, they were virtually all men way back then) who was in a farm practice, after which they decided to see the smaller companion critters. That is why we call it "small animal medicine." Look at the following habits and traditions, and the alternatives, and you may start to understand:

- We have routinely scheduled one doctor in one room with a single column of clients, yet physicians use four to six rooms per doctor and dentists are double that number. (Now think of the old time veterinarian, in the truck, doing one farm at a time.)

  ➤ If you believe in the new American Veterinary Practice, and understand that "staff produces the net," review High Density Scheduling concepts for some alternative methods.

- We have routinely charged anesthesia by the animal size, yet isoflurane costs ONLY about $6 per hour to use. (Now think of the value of the cow in the chute, the veterinarian and the black bag, and the cost per pound to make her well.)

  ➤ If you want the new American Veterinary Practice, consider this sequence, with each item/procedure deserving it's own fair price:
    ✓ pre-anesthetic blood screen (varies with age and physical condition),
    ✓ induction (less than $20, but covers most overhead),
    ✓ initial maintenance (not by weight, but for 30 minutes minimum),
    ✓ continuing anesthesia maintenance (by the minute),
    ✓ I.V. TKO (to keep open) —slow fluid drip,
    ✓ post-surgery pain medication,
    ✓ post-surgery hospitalization,
    ✓ then the follow-up plan.

- We have made pre-anesthesia blood screening voluntary and I.V. supportive therapy during surgery an exception because we are always asking "But what about the price????"

  ➤ In quality practices, the blood screen is mandatory now (as minimum and preferred "two yes" options).
  ➤ In progressive practices that worry about animal pain and rapid recovery, supportive I.V. therapy during surgery is mandatory.
  ➤ Post-surgical pain management is an "expectation" of most clients, yet it is forgotten by the provider due to "wallet medicine."

➤ Pricing is secondary to the "need" of the patient and the "need" of the provider in quality care. Compromise of professional standards is a liability.

• We have always charged hospitalization cage and run space by the animal size (almost like a feedlot operation).

➤ The value is in the time, process, and people involved, not in the kibble in the bowl:
  ✓ o.d./b.i.d. cases—level one hospitalization
  ✓ t.i.d./q.i.d. cases—level two hospitalization
  ✓ I.V. cases—level three hospitalization (also post-surgery)
  ✓ I.C.U. cases—level four hospitalization

➤ Yes, this can be used in bandaging (no joint, one joint, two joint, with an appliance or supportive wrap or without). Start rethinking your habits!

• We have always been afraid to sell our knowledge and instead have routinely sold "things" (e.g., vaccines at major inflation mark-ups, the cost of the "exam" instead of the "doctor's consultation," etc.).

➤ Producer veterinarians have started charging for their time, even time spent on the telephone, with clients.
➤ Producer veterinarians have started software computer systems to manage the husbandry for their clients, and they charge for this service.
➤ Producer and farm veterinarians charge by the mile to get to a client, yet specialists who travel between companion animal practices usually do not.
➤ When the pendulum swings, why do the companion animal veterinarians always wait for the "other guys" to change first?

• We have always managed companion animal practices by expense comparisons, yet the traditional veterinary software has been developed to resemble very fancy cash registers, tracking only income factors (and a mail merge for client mailings).

➤ Without expense-to-income relationships, you cannot determine net!
➤ Program-based budgeting (see Volume 2, *Building the Successful Veterinary Practice: Programs & Procedures*) provides program and procedure factors for managing practices—the things that make the front door swing!

➤ The new veterinary software systems, in 32-bit Windows technology, will track healthcare delivery, in picture and word, and the better systems will also have automatic data download to existing spreadsheet program capabilities for easy practice use.

So yes, Jack and Jane, money does matter, and it must be captured from the work we do. Veterinary medicine is a fee-for-service business, products are only supportive, and in companion animal practice, we generally treat patients that are considered "family members" (as shown in the original family value research published in *The Pet Connection*, CENSHARE, University of Minnesota). We deal in "needs," of the patient, the client, and the providers (which includes ALL staff members of a practice). Most of these factors are discussed in detail in Volume 2, *Building the Successful Veterinary Practice: Programs & Procedures,* so in this text, we will go beyond the day-to-day pricing and operations.

Annual "Program-Based" Budget

Budgeting is often a daunting activity, approached in some companies with a strange mixture of disinterest and awe.
—Robert G. Finney

The program-based budget lies at the absolute epicenter of practice activities, not as the driver, the dictator, or the demon but as the mile marker to success; it is like the score card of golf or the tote board at the race track—it is a fiscal-based score card that gives us the odds and handicapped assessment of success of our programs and procedures (see Volume 2 for greater elaboration). It exists not to beat down those around it but to serve as a standard of excellence. The program-based budget will provide targets and measurement for your vision and your expectations. While not every activity needs to make a "pure profit," the decision has to be yours; losses, on the other hand, should be avoided. When the Veterinary Chart of Accounts is married to the practice operations, you will begin to see the practice value you will need to maintain.

Line item accounting for expenses has always been done by traditional accountants, but they have ignored line items for income centers. This is called "dumb accounting" by everyone except the accountant sending you the bill (and these are the same people who seldom spell accounting with an "A"; their fees are often hidden from you under the categories of "legal" or "professional" because they alphabetize the P&L for their own benefit, not yours, and don't want to be at the top of the list). Even with nutritional product sales, one of the smallest mark-up activities in a practice, break-even analysis means you must know what is being spent and compare that to what is being sold—in real dollars! To know what is being sold, the beginning and ending inventory must be computed with the purchases to identify the real value of what was sold. This is what is compared to the nutritional product sales. With maintenance diets, a 20 to 25 percent net is expected, but with a heavy prescription diet program, 35 to 40 percent net is expected. Break-even analysis means ensuring the internal controls are adequate to maintain these levels of net. This is the level of managerial accounting needed for the best resale of a practice, although it is not needed for IRS tax accounting.

The budget-to-actual computations made each month are a combination of internal controls, break-even analyses, and quality assurance. The cost-per-use of a new piece of equipment is a form of break-even analysis, but a practice may not always be able to charge that much. The healthcare delivery team may use the cost-per-use as a method to establish a target for the number of times per month the practice must use the piece of equipment in order to break even (e.g., Idexx electrolyte machine, Vetronics ECG, endoscope, Biolog or Heska Lead II rhythm strip, ultrasound machine, a new dental base, etc.). Once the equipment-specific break-even point is determined, and the number of procedures computed to carry the cost is computed, every procedure exceeding this number is pure profit.

Beyond the $$$

Recognition and rewards require creative thinking. Consider the practice that allows one vacation day and 0.5 sick days per month; the only way to get the sick days is to stay home from work. Sickness, then, is a reward; attendance is not. Why not roll them all together and accrue "personal days" (e.g., one personal hour for every 20 scheduled hours worked) that can be taken for any reason, or collected as pay on an annual basis? How many practices surprise a salaried staff member with a gift certificate to say thanks after a very tough period (as with the prolonged disability absence of one of the key team members)? When was the last time someone in your practice received a three-day weekend just to acknowledge their sacrifice or team contribution? We even know one practice that sends their kennel master and his spouse on a three-day cruise to the Bahamas every January just as a thank-you for the holiday boarding effort.

Health programs are expensive, so we don't do them anymore.
—Anonymous

We practice good, innovative, creative medicine because no single treatment is appropriate in all cases. We could treat all our employees the same, except that the ever-present tax code has set up multiple obstructions to operations. We are mandated by our government to engage in the "Tax Avoidance Game." Even if we don't want to play, Uncle Sam takes our money. So we can either roll over and die and say, *"No way I can do that"* or we can take it on the chin and say, *"Health insurance is important to my people, times are hard; what more can I do to say thank-you?"*

One small incorporated business we consult with has created a "medical trust fund" that will pay a portion of health insurance premiums for its staff members. The fund is computed on a $1200 deductible policy, and it pays the deductible for two people on the policy. Using a "high deductible" health insurance policy results in massive savings. The policy pays for itself in six months if you save the difference in premiums. It is also owned by the staff member and is fully transportable. In addition, the payments are tax deductible to the company so the staff member does not get penalized for income; win-win occurs! It took this veterinary healthcare delivery company (practice) three years of nagging and prodding accountants, lawyers, and health insurance companies to find this procedure and put it into practice. The staff members appreciate the benefit, the practice appreciates the savings, and everyone appreciates the fact that the boss cared enough to make it happen.

Most communities have companies that specialize in economically supporting small business "cafeteria-style" benefit plans. Such plans allow a mixture of benefits, selected by vested/tenured staff members, based on a dollar ceiling established by a practice's budget. The pre-tax dollar benefit is important, especially in areas like dental care, ophthalmology needs, and day care.

One of the areas of practice that causes the most stress on practice and client alike is euthanasia. Are you reluctant to charge a fee at this time of sorrow? As an alternative, one practice encourages the client to write a check to a designated charitable agency. The practice then sends the check to the agency as a memorial to the pet, and the client receives a thank-you a few weeks later when the blues are cropping up again. Another practice has the euthanasia fee deposited into a *Pro Bono* fund that provides services to needy people, such as the kid with an HBC (hit by car) puppy or an ADG cat (ain't doin' good). At the end of the year, the contributors get a report of all the activities funded in memory of their pets. The Christian Veterinary Mission even has a fund to buy small livestock for third world development programs.

All of these benefits are important, but one of the largest potential areas for success in the staff benefit arena is trust. This simple trait is a benefit that pays great practice dividends. Trust means that you accept that every tenured employee cares about the practice, its clients, and providing a quality-based healthcare delivery to the patients. To understand this better, read the text, *Managing from the Heart*, by Bracey, Rosenblum, Sanford, and Trueblood, ISBN 0-385-30425-0, Delcorte Press. The basic premise of the text is a "caring heart" by the leader makes the team excel and the business more successful.

H Hear and understand each person.

E Even if you disagree, please don't make the other person wrong.

A Acknowledge the greatness within each person.

R Remember to look for the caring intentions for the ideas offered.

T Tell each person the truth with compassion.

These concepts are important, especially in healthcare. Practice managers plan, train, and motivate staff members within the perspective of the veterinarian's vision of the future. What makes them effective is the benefit the staff perceive when they see the practice leadership as competent, confident, and caring. A simple, easy-to-read text about this concept is *The Greatest Management Principle in the World (GMP)* by Michael LeBoeuf, Ph.D., 1985. *GMP* can be found in paperback in most bookstores. This text has often been quoted in veterinary practice management seminars, and frequently the author is not credited. Some of the ideas provided above stemmed from my reading or rereading of the *GMP* text. This insightful primer puts "benefits" into terms of quality, rewards, and action plans and allows the reader to become the leader, from within a practice team or from the top. Give some thought toward the paraprofessional staff in the veterinary practice where you spend most daylight hours of your life.

Lease or Buy?

"The credit purchase is the modern form of slavery."

The issue of capital expense equipment procurement is generally a problem for veterinary practices especially when looking at values during succession planning. The lack of cash budget compounds this issue, usually in a "must replace" situation. Practices that have the liquidity to pay cash for large purchases will generally pay the least for their equipment. However, excess cash may generate a better return on investment if used to retire high interest debt, promote the practice or increase services provided. The second distracter from purchasing equipment is the speed at which our profession is learning; much of "today's" equipment is already outdated tomorrow. The third distracter from purchase is the maintenance (also termed "owner tolerance") requirement; when you have "owned equipment," you also have the annoying problems that go with it.

For most veterinary practices, borrowing or leasing are the only viable choices for capital equipment procurement. Borrowing tends to be less expensive than leasing, unless it is done with high interest lines of credit or credit cards. Here, the credit worthiness of the practice, and the relationship with the local banker, can be a deciding factor. It is becoming a competitive banking world, and "shopping" for loan money is now an essential requirement when borrowing for equipment. Regardless of this effort, interest rates on equipment loans (collateralized) tend to be lower than interest rates on leases.

The "outside" equipment lease is not like an automobile lease; the residual value is seldom on your side! After three to five years the equipment has little resale value, so the practice pays close to the full cost of the equipment plus interest through the lease period.

If this description makes borrowing look better, consider the downside. When borrowing, you use a portion of your total credit line. This total credit line is often needed elsewhere. When purchasing equipment with borrowed money, you must have the "tolerance" to handle both the little problems and the obsolescence inherent in our technologically heavy profession. As the owner of a piece of equipment bought on credit, you might find that the new advances and applications are out of reach until the debt ratio is reduced.

The "internal" equipment lease is used to shelter money (e.g., gifting to a dependent child's education trust) or reduce practice value while maintaining personal liquidity. When equipment is placed into a separate L.L.C. or similar legal entity, it disappears from tangible assets of the practice's balance sheet, thereby lowering practice value and making the practice "easier to buy" because less of a down payment is required. The new L.L.C. leases the equipment back to the practice at a fair market value (FMV), and that lease money goes to the equipment owner without FICA, FUTA or other payroll-type taxes being matched by the practice. In the case of the gift to dependent children, depreciated equipment gifted can usually be depreciated again by the trust based on the FMV of the gift. This type of leveraging of internal equipment leases is why the local accountant and attorney must work closely with the practice ownership to maximize liquidity as well as tax benefits while developing the succession plan (three to five years of prior planning minimum).

As a quick overview of the procurement financing options, the following table is offered, including all three options:

. . . CASH . . .	. . . BORROWING . . .	. . . LEASING . . .
* Generally is the least expensive.	* Generally is less expensive than leasing.	* Protects you best from obsolescence.
* Enables practice to depreciate the equipment expense.	* Enables practice to depreciate the equipment expense.	* May not be a liability on the balance sheet.
But it . . . * Is in short supply at most practices.	But it . . . * Uses a credit line that could be used elsewhere.	But it . . . * Is the most expensive way to buy equipment.
* Might be better spent elsewhere in or for the practice.	* Exposes practice to risk of obsolescence. Midterm of lease.	* Carries penalties for cancellation.
* Exposes the practice to the risk of obsolescence.	* Represents a liability on your balance sheet.	* Provides 100% financing at a higher cost.

Other Factors

The banking industry is getting more conservative (translate this to being audited more often by the federal oversight agencies). More collateral, a greater percentage of "up front" money, and a closer look at the creditworthiness are the rules, not the exceptions, in today's banking world. In fact, John B. Stine II, a partner at Price Waterhouse, has stated, "Leasing has become more and more popular as bankers become increasingly conservative in lending to small businesses." Most leases are based on 100 percent financing, which probably explains why leased equipment grew at twice the rate of purchased equipment during the 1980s and into the 1990s. Since some companies will negotiate a lease payment schedule that is tied to seasonal cash flow trends, some leases have other advantages over a fixed rate loan. Many leases include an option to "trade up" or purchase the equipment at a fixed price in later years; this option is worth researching. The leasing of used equipment is also increasing, substantially reducing the practice procurement costs.

As a consultant, I have seen practices take leasing to extremes and become so lease heavy that the liquidity of the practice disappears. We have even encountered a consulting scam where the consultant has become the "middle man" in the leasing money cash flow and skimmed a "management fee" while sending the practice into major debt. Beware of this type of "helpful" consultant. In such cases, we often go to the banker and use the leased equipment as collateral to buy out the leases and establish a lower cost bank loan.

So which procurement option is best for you?

The key factors are a balance between 1) the practice's cash position, 2) the availability and cost of borrowing, and 3) the potential obsolescence of the equipment being considered. Practices with strong cash positions and good banking relationships seldom lease; rather, they are served best by borrowing and accelerating the repayment. With equipment that quickly becomes obsolete, a short-term operating lease allows greater practice flexibility. But for start-up practices or low cash flow practices with equipment that will remain viable for years, a long-term finance lease with a final residual payment will give the practice the lowest payment plus purchase option.

The Urge to Merge

There are risks and costs to a program of action, but
they are far less than the long-range risks and costs of
comfortable inaction.
—John F. Kennedy

As a consultant, what I have done in all mergers is become the
"Champion of the Outcome." This is the support model proven most
successful for human healthcare consultants. I have encountered "veterinary consultants" who fight for their client as if a merger was a win-
lose negotiation; this only causes failure to be built into the negotiations. With this in mind, this section is written from the "Champion of
the Outcome" perspective.

The Functioning Models

Almost all hospital merger models operating today are in human
healthcare. The simplest merger concept is that providers, facilities,
and financial systems come together to deliver quality healthcare. In
the early 1980s, hospitals formed HOLDING COMPANIES and gave
limited authority to a primary board that operated through multiple
levels of management oversight at multiple facilities. No one wanted to
give up any control. In the later 1980s, the holding companies evolved
into PARENT COMPANIES, with increased authority and a more
consolidated board structure, but still with multiple management
teams and diversified accountabilities. Control became centralized. In
the early 1990s, a SYSTEM ORIENTATION with central authority replaced the "parent company," most often with a single board and single management team. The "system" involved multiple hospitals and
other ancillary healthcare associated units to capitalize upon the
economies of scale available to the evolving group. There are many
permeations of these styles of merger models that are applicable to veterinary medicine. The precipitating factor is that inevitable evolution
cannot be stopped, but it can be guided. Also evident is that most
merger processes can be categorized into four definitive phases that can
be illustrated in a merger "**Process Flow Model**":

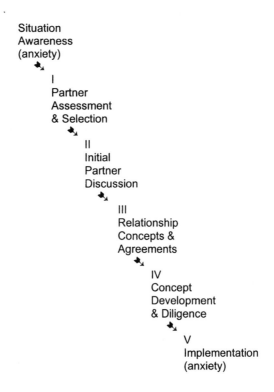

Situation
Awareness
(anxiety)

I
Partner
Assessment
& Selection

II
Initial
Partner
Discussion

III
Relationship
Concepts &
Agreements

IV
Concept
Development
& Diligence

V
Implementation
(anxiety)

The first critical question to be addressed is "Why merge?" What is the rationale for the concept? There are four factors that determine the answer: **market, cost, community,** and **system.** The **market** is geography-based in veterinary medicine and has impact on the share of market being enjoyed. The **cost** addresses economies of scale and the expense avoidance factors. The **community** is the benefactor of the consolidation and collaboration, when a quality and continuity of care ensues. The **system** of healthcare delivery becomes integrated, management develops into its own continuum, doctors become providers of healthcare services rather than managers of hospitals, and risk is diversified. These four factors arise from and have impact on the mission, vision, values, goals and objectives, and expectations for the merger evolution.

It is wise to note that anxiety is common to both the initial awareness of the merger need and the implementation of the merger. Phases I and II can generally be initiated without a consultant if the four basic "Harvard Rules of Negotiation" are followed:

1. Discuss interests but not positions,
2. Separate the people from the issues,
3. Seek creative solutions, and
4. Above all else, apply objective criteria.

As the key players enter Phase III, generally an objective and independent arbitrator will be required to "Champion the Merger Outcome." Phase III includes

✓ Definition of the mission,
✓ Clarity of vision,
✓ Identification of goals and objectives,
✓ Physical and operational structure planning,
✓ Power and control issues, and
✓ Climaxes with conflict resolution and a "letter of intent" between the key players.

Phase IV often requires the consultant but in some cases can be facilitated by a new hospital administrator hired by all the key players to ensure the success of the merger outcome. Phase IV explores the

✓ Opportunity quantifications,
✓ Business plan development,
✓ Task force interface,
✓ Organization model, and
✓ Actual merger documents which must precede the implementation.

There are four basic merger models, which range from greater autonomy to more centralized control:

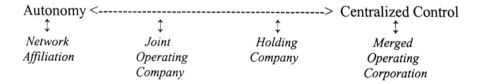

Autonomy <--> Centralized Control

| Network Affiliation | Joint Operating Company | Holding Company | Merged Operating Corporation |

Operational Concerns during Mergers

The legal entity of the merger could be a "C" corporation, an "S" corporation, a limited liability company (LLC), or some other emerging structure. (Because it varies by state or province, seek legal assistance from a qualified attorney with experience in professional healthcare legal entities.) Again, some loose guidelines should be followed, such as keeping the land and building outside the merged practice entity, although initially there may be common players in both groups. Over time, the owners of the merged practice will want to sell very small shares of the practice to allow a continuous ownership transfer to become the "standard" for the practice. The land and building may become assets of an estate. When the practice is separated and operated as its own entity does not matter. If in doubt during Phase I or II considerations, find out who owns the human healthcare facility in your community and how the local human hospital board is configured. Learn from those who have already done it!

The control of the new entity is vested in a "governance board," sometimes a large group, as with an emergency hospital, but more often in practice mergers (specialty groups or general practices), a smaller group, with a very basic one practice-one vote. The central issues of governance boards revolve around the questions of who, when, and how in both success and risk management situations. Once the board is established, the management philosophy must follow. This philosophy should include the hospital director authority, CEO requirements, the new hospital administrator position, degree of board involvement in daily operations (the less the better), and the new community profile.

The clinical and non-clinical consolidation of people, supplies and equipment sounds much easier than it is. The professional staff will merge, as will the paraprofessional staff, and these people must then deal with the daily healthcare delivery concerns. How will the new entity build on the existing human resource strengths? What effect will historical relationships play? What is the commitment level of EACH player? Can players meet most economic integration efforts planned by the new hospital administrator? And how will the traditional senior players feel when their original practice control mechanisms are eliminated (which is a requirement for success)? All of these concerns will be complicated by non-routine capital expenses, such as a new computer and fiscal management system for the merged entity.

After Phase I and Phase II discussions, the search for the "Champion of the Outcome" may be the most critical element of the merger process. There must be a common trust among the players. If all the players are not ready to compromise for the new entity, the process should not be started. The players should be realigned so those who remain are willing to release personal control and compromise for the good of the community and the new veterinary healthcare entity. Then the process should be started over. You <u>can</u> win!

A Dozen Signal Flares

"Most cash loss is due to trusted employees; if you didn't trust them, they wouldn't be handling the cash!"
—Dr. Cat

Internal controls in most veterinary practices are as weak as the internal controls in any family setting. This is to be expected but cannot be tolerated in succession planning! Most veterinary staff are paid as if they were adolescents on an allowance; the wage they receive isn't a retirement wage. Most people are hired onto the staff because they are nice people; they are trusted because trust is the most common element in the veterinary practitioner's way of life. Veterinarians don't see their practices as small businesses and do not approach the cash flow as if it needs to be controlled; they just want more cash flow. This attitude causes "adjustments" in most practice valuation formulas; therefore, for best economic results the formulas must be mediated for three to five years before the succession plan valuation begins.

Trust Everybody

After an embezzlement, information routinely provided to the insurance company includes the lack of time and/or business experience of the doctor; the limited number of employees (precluding segregation of function); whether the money was handled only by the receptionist team (but there was only one receptionist); the lack of generally accepted accounting practices (GAAP); and in most practices, the FAILURE of the accountant (CPA) to be involved in the internal controls and variance analysis of the practice's fiscal operations. Given these "excuses" and the potential most every practice has for lost cash, watch for these "signal flares," which indicate danger:

1. The receptionist operates with an open cash drawer (no receipts).
2. Receipts are made after the client departs, when there is "more time."
3. The receptionist never takes a vacation and is very protective of her turf.
4. The cash-handling person displays unexplained wealth, expensive vacations, new clothes, new jewelry, etc.
5. The petty cash fund (or worse, the change fund) contains IOUs instead of receipts (personal checks are also a warning sign here).
6. The money handler never asks for raises, takes a long time to cash paychecks, or never needs to leave early (during close-out) on days when she/he works alone.
7. The billing person rewrites invoices or records (allegedly for neatness), often working overtime after everyone else has left.
8. Accounting records are not up-to-date or must be taken home by an employee to close out the period.
9. Clients complain about errors in their statements or about a lack of a statement following a procedure/service.
10. Cash, as a percentage of total revenues, decreases each month, most often in direct relationship to the slowed practice growth.
11. The billing person gives vague reasons for writing off uncollectible accounts (or client accounts require more adjustments for error than in the past).
12. Staff members are not required to close out the change fund and balance against the daily receipts before departure (shortages and overages are accepted variances in daily activities).

Any of the above could occur normally in any practice. On the other hand, one or more could be a warning, a signal flare of danger. If one or more are detected, a thorough review of your cash collection system, billing system, and product procurement and distribution system is in order.

In God We Trust—All Others Pay Cash

Internal control is a system based on "segregation of function"— OR—the inability of any one person to have control of all the steps in the process. For instance, someone orders supplies, a different person receives the items and checks off the shipping documents as "received." That person then gives the annotated documents to the doctor who, in turn, transmits them to the person who pays the bills. If a computer system is in use, every client should be logged through the appointment log (even walk-ins), assigned a circle sheet (travel sheet) for the visit (even over-the-counter sales), and logged out through the computer. In the absence of a computer system, a one-write receipt system should be in effect to serve a similar purpose.

Your accountant should be able to assist you in determining an appropriate internal control system that uses a common sense, staff dependent, segregation of function. If the accountant can't or won't help you (or wants to charge an extra fee), call a practice consultant who specializes in veterinary practice management, knows the American Animal Hospital Association's (AAHA) Chart of Accounts, and can help establish a practice-specific internal control system. The peace of mind alone is worth the investment. Quality veterinary practice consulting resources will usually offer the initial telephone consultation to a veterinary practice owner at no cost. There is no reason to remain at risk; act now, before it is too late for someone you trust.

Without a yardstick, there is no measurement. Without measurement, there is no control. Without control, there is no business expectation for the practice. Without a business expectation for the practice, there is no way to measure practice business excellence.
—Dr. Cat

Practice Valuation

You have done everything to build a viable, expansive practice with people who are excited about the quality of medicine being provided and about the knowledge that you are the standard in your community and among your colleagues. Now you look ahead and wonder just what you have built. What is your practice worth in the cold morning light of the marketplace? Appendix A offers two methods to calculate this value.

Unfortunately, the simplest answer is also the most complex. An accountant will tell you the value of your practice is the sum of the assets and the net earnings that result from the exercise of the assets. Then he or she will tell you the street value of the building, the equipment, the cash, and the inventory. The accountant will also tell you that the amount of money left over last year when all the legitimate and reasonable expenses are paid can also be "sold" (given the correct conditions, period of transition, economic conditions of the community, "competition" from your beloved colleagues) ... until you say "Whoa back, mule. What about goodwill?"

And he/she says, quietly, looking you right in your steely-grey lights, "There is no Goodwill." And the CPA is not smiling. And you realize that the world doesn't take heed of the 20 years you spent 80 hours a week building the practice. Because a buyer won't care. All that counts is what you actually did for your time, how you did it, and what net did your business show each year in the recent past.
—Dr. Rob Deegan

While the practice value is based on the cold, hard logic of the money talking, it is the steps you took to get to the place you are that will determine what you have. Can you believe it? All those years what "they" were telling you was wrong. So, one more time, what are the assets you have in the practice of medicine? The Three Ps of asset assessment are

Practice Place. This is the facility and all that equipment that will show up as a line item in the practice valuation.

People. This is all the staff: the veterinarians, the paraprofessionals, and the other support staff down to and including maintenance and animal caretakers. And, as you know, those are the only kinds of people you have working for you. (We do hope you didn't skip the ISUP trilogy, *Building the Successful Veterinary Practice*, to rush to this text.) Plus, those pesky clients . . . dare we say they are your most valuable and vital asset? You bet!

Posterity. How intently did you look to the future? How heavily did you invest in your dreams and the dreams of your compatriots? These efforts on your part will show up every day in the operations of the practice: the outpatient nurses who translate your gross into practice net; those who convert a good diagnosis into quality patient care; those who increase surveillance of any deferred or symptomatic care case; those who convert your practice philosophy into active follow-up (Recall, Recheck, Remind).

The picture of the practice value that emerges hinges on the effective utilization and potentiation of the resources: human, capital, and material. How the practice has promoted training and expanded the role of all staff, how the practice has supported the individual growth of knowledge and skills, how attitude has been maintained, and the environment of the healthcare delivery system all influence the practice value.

All the past resource utilization shows up on the valuation, but the value develops quietly for a long time before most practitioners want to ask for it back. Most owners do not even understand their own balance sheets. Take a look at the valuation concepts in Appendix A and see how all the factors of leadership, management, and quality healthcare delivery figure into the equation.

The Value of the Practice Is the Sum of Tangible Assets, Client Records, and the Net Excess Earnings

The first asset on the list is **Real Estate**. The practice might actually own the land and building, but more and more we are seeing veterinarians who (for good reason) own the building outside of the fiscal practice structure. If they do, the practice has a leasehold improvement asset that depreciates over time, and the practice pays rent instead of a mortgage. Real estate needs a professional appraisal on a timely basis, this appraisal, of course, is subject to the swings of the local economy. Don't guess on this. And be sure the appraiser understands that a veterinary practice is, by necessity, the best use of a veterinary facility.

Inside the building are the bits and pieces and tools of the trade. This **Equipment** is essential to the operation of the practice and comes in a wide variety of ages and quality. The most honest value of equipment is by replacement value. This is the cost of getting another piece of equipment to do the same job. (The pre-owned equipment market has ESCALATED in the 1990s, so values are easier to ascertain.) You may use your records to arrive at this figure or hire a knowledgeable and profession-specific individual. The critical issue is the purpose of assessing the value. If the value is to be used for a sale outside the practice, a more rigorous and definable process needs to be applied. For internal use among consenting adults, as with partnership or other practice management issues, jointly establishing an internal value is quite appropriate.

A piece of equipment may be so old that you can't get another like it, or none of the newer generation equipment can perform that task. (This is a clue, by the way, that your medical skills need attention.) If no replacement is available, the equipment probably has no value.

Another consideration is how much life is left in a piece of equipment. It is necessary to "discount" the replacement value according to expected longevity. Equipment that is over two years old and is therefore subject to rapid wear, tear, and obsolescence is valued at about 60 percent of the replacement value. On the other hand, equipment without moving parts that is made of solid stainless steel and has a reputation for very long life is often worth almost 80 percent value.

In addition to the equipment, there is **Inventory**. Inventory consists of the consumable supplies, from paper towels to antibiotics to set-ups for the blood chemistry machine. The real practice inventory control program, either computerized or hand maintained, will give a very close approximation of the value (no system = minimal value). Often a simple "touch-each-thing" count is all that is needed for valuation. If the practice is complying with taxation requirements, a wall-to-wall inventory of all expendable property is conducted at least annually to check on the flow of materials.

Inventory has a maximum value for about six months. The economic turnover in this economy precludes holding on to consumables any longer. Count anything older than 6 months as a value of zero. (Use it or lose it!)

Frequently all or some of the above have an attached **Liability** in the form of a debt, mortgage, lease, or loan. A liability is in itself a tool of business, as previously discussed, and is not to be shunned. Though debt may be as dangerous as a scalpel in a kindergartner's paw, it is also a thing of beauty and art in the hands of a surgeon. You are interested in the long-term amount of principle due. The current cost, both interest and current principle, is a matter of **Expense**.

The most notable and observable asset is **Cash**. This asset, or lack of it, is the primary cause of practitioners berating their accountants or calling on consultants. Cash may be sitting in a bank account or be in the form of a short-term note. It may be in a mason jar in the biologics refrigerator, or it may be on the books as accounts receivable (please note, the tax man likes this asset, so keep it small) with a modest discount for the deadbeat fringe who will not pay (less than 1 percent annual write-off is an acceptable tolerance). Cash also has its own liability set-off; it is called accounts payable.

Your valuable **Clients** (all of them) may be quantified using higher mathematics such as adding, subtracting and multiplying. The client who gives you a lot of business in a year is fiscally more significant to your practice than the one who comes in every third year for Fluffy's rabies vaccination. *No single client can be quantified in monetary terms.* Please read that again—it is very important. And please remember that the most important clients you have are the ones you are looking at every day—your staff!

For valuation statistics, however, you may characterize your client base and assign a value to the entire base (as described in Appendix A of this book). The factors that apply here are the Average Client Transaction (ACT), the Retention Rate of clients in your practice, the one-year Present Value of Future Earnings, the "Class of Return Rate" for the client base, and the number of clients in each class.

Net Excess Earnings is the final measurement of the practice value. The assets are static on their own; how the practice uses the assets determines if the practice entity remains operational, providing quality medicine and peace of mind to a lot of swell people. After all the bills are paid and equipment replaced as needed, there is a measurement called "Profit." Profit is frequently given different names and measured differently under different circumstances (so buyer beware). It may very well be that a practice owner has one number for buddies at the AVMA convention and another for the IRS (bless their souls). The difference is the "art" of practice valuation!

Having an innovative and creative accountant is a good thing, but this person needs to work for the practice, not just the computer. The first report generated in the valuation process should be the practice's cash flow situation. A sole owner may feel that his or her profit is what is left over after everybody else is paid. This owner may hold title to the real estate under a private mortgage. All this is fine for daily operations ... but when the practice has to pay all clinicians' salaries, pay all rent, and provide reasonable operating expense monies, the formula for computing profit becomes clouded. What is left after people and overhead are "paid," regardless of how the accountant reports the cash flow, is the true "net profit"; this is the Net Excess Earnings. Net Excess Earnings is often confused with the **Return on Investment** (ROI), but here again, different accountants may calculate this differently. Don't let them confuse the numbers beyond the understanding of the ownership. The Net Excess Earnings is the money left over AFTER everything else is paid. It is the money available for reinvestment or for paying off liabilities. It is the money a new owner has to pay the debt of practice procurement. This amount is the measure of the financial success of the practice.

We have encountered a practice with close to $600,000 in gross sales but only $14,000 in excess earnings. Consider this statement closer: the practice is doing business but has only $14,000 at the end of the year to re-invest. This is an extreme example, but it is not unique in our experience. This practice entity, in effect, has a value of only $39,000 (not much compared to the value of the assets), and the size of the gross is moot. To reiterate: the value of the practice is the "value of the assets" plus the Net Excess Earnings of the practice over a measurable near future.

The Trail is the thing, not the end of the trail. Travel too fast and you miss all you are traveling for.
—Louis L'Amour

Alternative Methods

Discussions with most accountants reflect a failure to evaluate the practice philosophy and scope of services for the veterinary facility under study. These factors have an influence within any actual evaluation of a practice's demographic and goodwill potentials. An on-site, in-depth veterinary professional evaluation can be conducted by a few veterinary practice consultants, if certain assumptions are based on a statistically valid medical record audit and first-hand observations. At Veterinary Practice Consultants® (Catanzaro & Associates, Inc.), there is even an internal "snapshot" valuation provided to clients for less than $1000, but it is not an on-site and can only be used for friends and partners, not legal conflicts. Legal conflicts REQUIRE an on-site validation for valuation purposes (which is a more expensive valuation process). The "snapshot" alternative, as well as using the Appendix A alternative valuation protocols, may even help to determine practice philosophy and scope of services. These "simplified systems" are much "friendlier" to the internal assessment process (adjustments = excuses). When the valuation is for use between a buyer and seller, we believe a veterinary medical record audit is REQUIRED, either as part of the valuation, or as a concurrent assessment. The audit generally reflects a documentation shortfall when compared to the "stated" practice philosophy.

The traditional approach to veterinary practice valuations has been the cost approach, the direct sales comparison, and the income approach. When a CPA or other valuation "expert" compares these three alternatives, certain basic healthcare delivery assumptions must be understood:

- In veterinary medicine, we believe the income approach to be invalid because there are no comparable income methods for veterinary hospitals (reference Owen McCafferty, CPA, Veterinary Economics, circa 1987). Gross income capabilities, vacancy rates, and collection losses are not applicable; capitalization rates are practice-specific, not community-based.
- The direct sales approach is not appropriate because there are no comparable real estate holdings that would be sold on a consistent basis for veterinary hospitals. No valid method to adjust prices exists since veterinary healthcare facilities must be built for better quality and more durability, have higher electrical and plumbing capabilities and multiple HVAC systems, as well as other profession-specific requirements due to animal handling, sterile surgery, and client service requirements.
- The cost method has most often been the best method to use in veterinary medicine because it reflects the value of the asset, especially since the land and physical facility is valued based on the actual cash values. A practice resells to another veterinarian based on the "Net" of the practice as well as the location. The cost approach reflects the value of organizing a veterinary practice from scratch and reflects transactional impacts, while the other two methods ignore the "social contract" associated with the business of veterinary medicine.

The most used practice valuation formula in the veterinary profession has been the 1987 *Veterinary Economics* system by Owen McCafferty, CPA. McCafferty based the description on factors that are significant in the veterinary medical profession. The August, September, and October 1987 issues of *Veterinary Economics* provided one of the very best descriptions of the valuation process and parameters, in the hands of a skilled accountant who could "adjust" the individual expense factors for reasonable professional trends and real forecasted values (this statement excludes most evaluators). To elaborate on the elements of concern and use of the formula; the reader must take special note of the importance of the "historical net" AS WELL AS the need to "adjust" expense factors to industry standards. The fact that it took three issues to describe makes it evident that it is not an easy concept. Besides, in addressing the problems inherent with any capitalization rate formula, more than one CPA has used the formula improperly because they do not know the veterinary medicine profession.

As you can see, these formats of fiscal self-assessment can lead to a complex financial planning problem. To use only your own resources to solve the investment picture is silly. You have bankers, brokers, accountants, and financial planners on your client list whom you trust and who will work for your benefit with their expertise. Cultivate the resources available to you, and program your financial future as you would your practice growth. Know exactly where you want to be next year, in three years, and in five years from a practice perspective and a financial goal system. If you don't know when or where you want to retire, set some general business and practice goals to help establish the retirement or resale potential that could be measured and evaluated within the one-three-five year goal-setting program.

The experience of Catanzaro and Associates, Inc., points to one inestimable action an owner can take to maintain practice value: prior planning! Appendix A provides valuation formats to help monitor the practice value progress; use one of them annually. Most single practitioners expect to find a "buyer" when the time is right to sell. Most practitioners don't plan for it, and therefore, few find the right buyer, at the right time, with the right amount of money, to close the deal. Therefore, succession planning is critical for capturing the value of the asset called a "practice."

Succession Planning

Succession planning does not have to wait for reorganization of the practice, or reconstruction of the facility, or expansion of the Net, or even the growing enfeeblement of "Old Doc." All plans can proceed simultaneously. Concurrently, failure to establish a succession plan is the primary disaster indicator for practice value. Reality: most larger practices now sell to somebody inside the practice. Careful nurturing of associates in medical services, strong vision-based leadership, and fiscal responsibility are essential to take advantage of this most valuable asset. An associate who has been hired with some form of "buy-in option" needs to see how the plan will unfold and at what times certain decisions will be made by both parties. Associates who do not make the grade as partners need to be placed on another track.

Since not all sales will be to associates, it is necessary to nurture other options. Build the "competition" into colleagues, and colleagues into friends. When the time comes, these people will be more likely to be on your side than total strangers will. In the end, a seamless transition, totally unnoticed by your clients, will preserve net earnings, client records, inventory, equipment, sanity, and hope.

Herewith are a few guidelines to start planning and discussion. Some of these are common sense, but none of these is a "rule of thumb" because we hate dumb thumb rules.

- Practice sale preparations need to start at least three years BEFORE the anticipated separation date, since net must be increased (every valuation formula is "net sensitive").
- Actually, five years before, smart sellers quit laundering money (hiding expenses and salaries) through the practice, and then, in the fourth year, they establish a growth and promotion plan that will cause a growing practice profile over the next half-decade.
- The banks and other lenders will NOT lend money on goodwill, projected earnings, etc. Projected earning value will have to be addressed in a down payment unless you are going to carry the paper.
- Building and land is best in a separate "land and cattle company" (an LLC, family trust, or some other shelter) and you NEED to be paying (yourself) a reasonable rent (e.g., 7-10%). And yes, this saves federal taxes every month as well as at the end of the career, especially if the "real estate entity" is not within the practice owner's estate.
- If the practice is solely owned and has multiple associates, consider a junior partner with your tenured professional team for a stair-step purchase option, which allows small shares to be systematically purchased by the favored doctor over a prolonged period of time.
- If the practice has many partners and few associates, ensure that you have some form of "first death" protection insurance. The ownership of the policy should belong to a legal entity other than yourself (thereby keeping the proceeds out of the $600,000 estate tax), and

the beneficiary needs to be kept current (and, again, it should not be the practice entity for estate and taxation reasons).

- The old valuation system of taking the annualized average of three years' gross as the practice price is valid ONLY if: 1) the practice has experienced a 20 percent net growth annually, 2) there is no debt, AND 3) someone is willing to buy it at that price (a rare combination in today's buyer market). The "70-80 percent of gross" thumb rule is becoming a closer approximation of the average companion animal practice, which is at the 9-15 percent net income growth level, as discussed earlier, but please remember this is affected by debt, assets and community demographics (which we will discuss in Chapter 2).

- Specialty practices and production livestock practices have a value in real assets but little else; reputations carry these practices. Therefore, some form of partnership and/or shared ownership is essential for increasing their value at retirement.

- The transition of ownership and practice leadership should be initiated at least a full business cycle before the anticipated retirement date, since the practice's leadership must be transferred smoothly for the purpose of staff and client retention. This often requires a mediator (a qualified consultant and mentor) to assist all parties and maintain the harmony and practice pride (quality is what the clients call pride).

- If you are a young practitioner, start banking/investing 10 percent of your take-home every month, effective immediately, with NO excuses. If you are an older practitioner or tenured staff member, you should ALREADY be doing the same!

- Also, at the end of every year, whether you are a practice owner or a productivity-based associate getting an end-of-year bonus, place 50 percent of the excess net into solid real estate investments in your own community. In this manner, practice sale becomes supplemental money, not primary retirement income.

These points are being made here simply because too many practices fail to plan ahead—and **the public veterinary corporations are NOT always the answer.** If you cannot see your practice days ending or you see only one method of exit, then succession planning is even more critical. Succession planning is how to move from one point of your veterinary medical evolution to the next level of life. It needs to be done today, and committed to completely, regardless of the evolutionary point you are at, since life and family are long-lasting , while practice is transitory. Today is already yesterday's tomorrow, and nothing stopped it from happening. Learn from that fact. Plan for the future, and it won't be scary.

The leadership instinct you are born with is the backbone. You develop the funny bone and the wishbone that go with it.
—Elaine Agather

Risks and Demographic Demands

2

Traditionally, practice valuations have ignored community demographics, mainly because a decade ago it was not a critical factor. As we enter the new millennium, the community demographics critically affect practice value and, therefore, affect succession planning and strategic response to community dynamics.

Assessing the Competitive Environment

Your colleagues in other veterinary practices are not against you; they are merely for themselves.
—Dr. T. Catanzaro

Demography is the study of population statistics or, in the case of veterinary practices, an external environment to blame for internal trends. For succession planning, demography is also an assessment of internal population dynamics; the practice is a community of healthcare delivery people. Both aspects will be considered in this chapter because any change in external or internal demographics will modify the healthcare delivery protocols that form the foundation of any veterinary practice's value.

Hardly a sector of our economy is unaffected by demographic change. Education has had to cope with declining enrollment in elementary and secondary schools, colleges have begun to feel the effects of fewer students, and more veterinarians (baby boomers) compete for fewer clients. While demographics and social changes have caused rising demands for some veterinary procedures (increased cat and bird ownership), and decreasing demands for others (poultry or family farms), our profession's own lack of business activity has compounded the challenges. Now, and into the new millennium, we can no longer blame others or the community for our own practice's failure to meet the needs of the catchment area (those animal owners in proximity of the practice). Clients will not leave a practice that meets their needs.

Veterinary practice success is also surprisingly simple to achieve, according to many of the current speakers and authors. As a practice consultant, I do not believe that is necessarily the case. The number of variables that impact a practice makes the success process anything but simple. In working with a consulting team, a model was developed to describe the challenges facing most veterinary practices today; that model follows. The easiest illustration possible appears be a hypothetical case study of a "flat line" veterinary practice, an occurrence we are asked to respond to more frequently as the community practice densities increase.

To put the critical practice success factors into a modern assessment perspective, the model illustrated has been developed for use during consultation engagements. The three-dimensional was originally a problem-solving model, but it is also a risk assessment model. If challenges cannot be addressed, risk goes up and value goes down. If a practice modality can be adjusted, the challenge is diminished, as is the risk. These are leverage factors for the capitalization note in most every traditional valuation formula but are seldom addressed by average accountants or unknowing valuation experts. It is hoped that the case study will make the model matrix come alive for the reader.

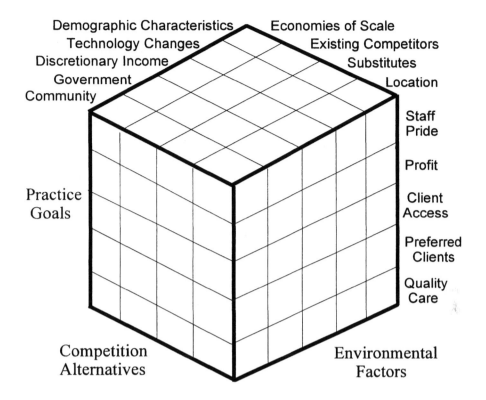

Demographic Characteristics   Economies of Scale
Technology Changes   Existing Competitors
Discretionary Income   Substitutes
Government   Location
Community

Staff
Pride

Profit

Practice
Goals

Client
Access

Preferred
Clients

Quality
Care

Competition
Alternatives

Environmental
Factors

The Challenge Presented

The practitioner calls and says the gross has flattened out this year; the 10 to 20 percent annual growth rate has disappeared from the practice. He has tried newsletters to no avail, and the sequence of three reminder cards has only gotten a 50 percent response rate.

A pet food discount center has opened within five miles and the local humane society has added a spay and neuter clinic, subsidized by a community benefactor. To make matters worse, the staff turnover has been 100 percent each year. The practitioner wants to know if he should pay $15,000 to $20,000 for an outside (generic program, developed outside the veterinary profession) consulting firm's assistance.

The Three Dimensions

A reality check is in order for this practice. The multiple factors that impact the success have been defined in terms of the competition, but the ability to react is not within the practice's experience. The model provided is a form of an integrated checklist that allows the practice leadership to assess each observed or perceived factor against the environment, competition, and internal practice concerns. This is essential for practice growth, whose "potential" affects the capitalization rate!

The major assessment factors for companion animal veterinary practices have been interrelated in the three-dimensional model because keying into the required competitive elements impacting any given practice is not that simple. Also, given any "excuse" for poor performance, it can be followed around the "Rubik's Cube®" and assessed from many alternative perspectives that cross the issues. Some elements may appear perfect when considered within themselves (e.g., location) until we compare them to another dimension of consideration (e.g., new zoning codes). I have labeled the three dimensions

- Environmental Factors
- Competitive Factors
- Goals of the Veterinary Practice

Each of these dimensions has been subdivided into major elements of consideration that are usually found to apply to most veterinary practices. Alternative elements, or additional elements, may be added when assessing your own situation. Each element used in the example will be briefly discussed within the case scenario to allow the reader to better understand the assessment impact(s).

Environment Axis

This axis will influence the performance of any practice or all practices. Owners of most veterinary practices have resigned themselves to the fact that they can't change their environment, but few have looked at how to use their environment to their advantage. While we cannot change the environmental factors, we can adapt to them; when we fully understand the interrelationships, we can let them work to our advantage.

The demographics of any locality always change, and with the Chamber of Commerce adaptation of the national census, information will become available in many forms. The Chamber of Commerce in your community wants additional businesses to enter their tax base, so their assessment forecasts are often "proactive," but regardless, the data is compatible to the average veterinary practice's needs (e.g., resources available per community group). In the case of the flat line practice, an upper middle-class subdivision had expanded just one mile across the interstate, but the practice hadn't made any effort to target this group (demographics) with a quality statement (patient care and client relations) that explained why residents should visit the practice. We found a local Boy Scout troop that would deliver custom-designed Earth Day litter bags (with an environmental practice message inside) to every doorknob at half the price of bulk mail (substitutes)!

Technology constantly changes (e.g., isoflurane), which sometimes helps the practice but often causes additional costs that were not figured into the long-range budget. Spays and neuters had never made the flat line practice money (profit), but the owner of the practice thought they had developed extra clients. A record review showed that those clients who took advantage of the low cost services (low discretionary income) seldom became four-visits-a-year clients (economies of scale), and seldom added to the practice's new referred client list (client relations). The ability to cross-sell to these low discretionary income clients was never developed because the flat line practice did not believe in that style of internal marketing; flat line decided to put their patient care efforts into other health care endeavors that would differentiate the practice from the competition.

The government always impacts veterinary practices with zoning, taxes, legislation, and other headaches. We obtained a Chamber of Commerce ten-year community planning map and saw that an outpatient clinic could be economically established in a newly zoned expansion area on the northern edge of town (15 minutes from the present facility). This new facility would help discourage new and existing competitors and increase the economies of scale for the inpatient services offered by the existing facility. It also allowed the flat line practice to put its tenured associate into a new, growing practice (self-worth) and share time between the two facilities (economies of scale), while keeping a central supply and personnel management system at the parent facility (lower cost).

The community contains our greatest fixed expense (occupancy and staff costs) but concurrently holds the greatest variable that affects the net income (client source). The staff of the flat line practice was hired at below its local McDonald's starting salary, not given pay raises during the initial training year, and had no idea what the salary would be after a year. We changed the hiring wage to match McDonald's for untrained personnel and matched assistant department manager wages at the local Sears or Penney's for the experienced staff. When we matched these "suppliers" and gave a 90-day raise (self-worth) after successful completion of the introductory employment period and a raise at 180 days, the employees gained a feeling of belonging and appreciation. They treated the clients the way they were treated (client relations), and the client bonding (return visits and phone calls for assistance) to the practice increased.

Competition Axis

The second axis of the matrix will affect and be affected by the environmental factors. The heart of any competitive strategy is to relate the organization to the environment. Veterinary schools continue to graduate veterinary students at a number in excess of the veterinarian mortality rate; practices continue to hire these new graduates at wages low enough to force them to open their own practices after they become trained and established within the community.

In the area of our flat line practice, the number of practices within three miles to the south had doubled in the past five years. This meant that the full-time-equivalent veterinarian-carrying capacity of the catchment area (location) had been saturated but that competition from within the profession continued to increase. The new satellite option to the north provided the existing staff a place to work while expanding the client catchment area (usually those pet owners within 15 minutes from the practice's door). The 1990s was also the decade of the service industry, and this flat line practice saw expanded competition (e.g., PetsMart®) within the ancillary and adjunctive areas of the veterinary practice. In a recessionary time, increased service (accessibility), maintained or increased advertising, and increased training for the staff increased the practice's competitive edge.

Economies of scale describe the cost effectiveness seen with the flat line practice assuming the central procurement functions, allowing specialization of the paraprofessional and professional staff, and networking the healthcare facilities. While "substitutes" describe those industries that have expanded in the ancillary veterinary product markets, such as nutritional centers, pharmacies, feed stores, mail order, groomers, kennels, pet stores, and a host of other convenience delivery systems, the term also applies to the concept of the flat line practice's "veterinary extender program." This is where the paraprofessional staff assumed duties as nutritional or behavior counselors, inventory managers, and management associates (also a new member classification established with the American Animal Hospital Association) to allow the veterinarians more patient healthcare contact time and, thus, greater income. The veterinarians of the practice still produced a similar gross, but the paraprofessional staff increased the net.

Location was a competitive factor in the early days of the practice, but the infusion of competition took away the exclusivity of the location. At the flat line practice, we target-marketed to the elderly population by promoting the central location, the private parking lot, and the longer appointment periods. The length of time the practice had been in the community was added to the cover of the practice brochure. Owners of the practice realized that without target marketing and tailoring of services, the location concerns would become an environmental factor.

Suppliers can affect our costs as well as our delivery of products; with the recessionary trend, flat line started to pay vendors cash on delivery, thus strengthening its bond with the most dependable vendors. A consequence was achieving better supplier alternatives (e.g., cheapest cost for annual orders with monthly shipments and billings) that allowed greater practice efficiency.

The existing competitors were redefined as colleagues of the flat line practice; a specialist was brought in weekly for all the veterinarians in the community to use. Colleagues come in many forms, and the veterinarians responded with a spectrum of rational and irrational responses; those who used the specialist found they did not lose clients, and they gained a higher quality of medicine. In our assessment of the competition's impact on the profession, the flat line practice raised the quality of care, the client veterinary I.Q., and their total cash flow by introducing a specialist consulting service.

Goals Axis

The third axis of the matrix represents the traditional commitments of veterinary practice and is used to formulate competitive strategies for finding a position that exploits the strengths and minimizes the weaknesses of a practice. Most of the efforts of the flat line practice have been discussed in the previous practice examples, but there are a few additional factors to understand.

The goals of the flat line practice were written with many intermediate objectives that were measurable and attainable. The Five-year Business Plan, the Budget Targets, and the annual Marketing Plan were all forms of goals that drove the objectives the staff members had targeted for action. Every objective discussed with any staff member was evaluated by the C-R-A-M method: accepted as a *challenge* to the individual, *realistic* for their current skill and knowledge level, *attainable* for the practice within the time specified, and *measurable* by some pre-selected objective or quantitative method (often a date).

The flat line practice changed its performance appraisal system to a 90-day system of objectives aimed at quarterly, semi-annual, and annual goals. Each day started with managers reviewing a list of critical practice goals to meet the weekly goals and objectives. Goal setting had to be done from the perspective of the practice philosophy, so a brief statement that captured the dream and shared the vision of the veterinarian was developed. Note that any interaction of factors in the other two axes will usually result in a need to adjust the roles and goals of the practice to these three commitments.

Quality patient care encompasses the scope of services offered by a practice and varies with the practitioner. At the flat line practice, we standardized this by developing a technical manual to describe the most common expectations for quality health care delivery. Higher levels of quality inpatient care are often not as profitable as outpatient services, but this trade-off was made in light of environmental perceptions (ability to pay) and client relations (differentiation of the practice from the competitors). The profit motive was germane to keeping the doors open and, as such, was a critical element used to weigh other dimensions. It was discovered that 64 percent of the clients had dual income families, so the practice's hours were adjusted to meet the client's perceived needs. Concurrently, a day drop-off healthcare service was initiated for "established clients" to reduce the waiting problems; this was then cross-sold as an added benefit of being a return client.

A personal and positive feeling of self-worth is critical to prevent the "burn-out syndrome," another 1980s phrase that usually describes boredom or frustration. The excitement of the new outpatient facility, the weekly specialist visit, and the increased inpatient care program changed the attitude of the flat line practice staff.

Strategic Responses

If these three axis elements are seen as potentially flexible in the practice goal setting dimension, then we have factors that can be used to impact the other dimensional factors and capitalization rate. Knowing the factors does not always provide the alternatives; this is the com-

petitive environment where good consultants earn their fees. I work
with a team of practice consultants who see over 200 quality practices
a year and glean many great ideas from what works and doesn't work;
this is often the basis for establishing a selection of alternatives. In the
following paragraphs, several strategies that hospitals use, or could
use, to respond to their changing environments, competition, or practice values are examined.

Diversification. The benefit of offering more services is a potential
added source of revenue, spreading some of the financial risks and
cross-subsidizing financial losers. The downside is losing perspective
on the quality of medicine required to support a long-range, loyal
client base. The major impact we have seen relates to quantity factors, more outpatient emphasis, greater community expansion programs, and dilution of the traditional quality healthcare priorities.

Vertical Integration. The self-insuring health maintenance agreements,
as well as the use of third-party insurance systems, are a good example of the vertical integration strategy. These programs increase
control over financing veterinary care and often attract/maintain inpatient loyalty. The downside is the increase of price competition for
care, which hurts the community level of care. Major impacts in securing the loyal clients to the practice for the run of the agreement
and handling cost inquiries from non-users have been seen.

Horizontal Integration. With the merging of competitors, we see such
benefits as the economies of scale from multiple facilities, the restriction of client erosion from other practices, and the management
of local competition. On the downside, multiple facilities require the
attention of an astute manager and different leadership styles based
on the players within the outlying facilities; clients have a tendency
to shift between practices, expecting similar levels of care. The major impacts we have seen are that "equitability" is much more difficult to achieve and alliance factors complicate the management efforts.

Joint Venture. The use of this vehicle to raise capital and minimize financial risks has been a benefit trend. The downside is a loss of the
traditional control of the practice to experts in profit and loss. Impact factors are especially harsh on the traditional commitments
(goals) of the veterinary profession.

Marketing. The benefits of marketing are related to attracting and

maintaining clients, developing not only an awareness, but also a
higher client veterinary I.Q., and the complementing use of other
strategies. The detractors are those practices that cannot differentiate between advertising, merchandising, marketing, and the
client benefit. We see an impact on the client/patient mix, the spectrum of services, and the colleague interrelationships within a
community.

Political Action. The benefits of preventing or encouraging legislation
that affects all areas of veterinary practice are obvious. The downside is the financial responsibilities of supporting a PAC or lobbyist,
the isolationist tradition of the veterinary practitioner, and the perception of the small effect the profession has on the community. The
major impacts are related to class action agreements between practices and legislative awareness of the profession.

Internal Efficiency. The benefit of systems that monitor and reduce the
use of resources to cut costs while still meeting client demands has a
place in every practice. The downside is that personnel are often
overworked and underpaid, corners are cut in healthcare delivery,
and quality is reduced to save pennies. The impact of this approach
is seen in the increased use of veterinary extenders within the practice and the employment of practice consultants to gain better ideas
on efficiencies available.

Bottom Line

This matrix model and the accompanying descriptions are meant as
an overview of the marketplace assessment considerations of the new
millennium as well as practice valuations. The profession has left the
days of the "quick-fix" and must now realize the strong interrelationships that control the practice's reflex to gimmicks and special events.
The use of three reminders, a computer invoice, or a newsletter is no
longer what makes the significant difference, but rather, how these factors fit into the assessment matrix model of interrelationships, how
practice programs are adjusted, and the commitment to set quality
healthcare delivery procedures to make the "business" less of a risk.

It is my belief that each practitioner has the capabilities to manage
and assess the practice, but the tools he or she needs to do so are not
available. Maybe this explains why we get referrals from valuation

agents who want us to do a practice consultation to increase net BE-FORE they continue their quest for sale. This is also why we call it "succession planning" rather than buy-sell; it takes planning, programs, and time to improve the capitalization rate. If a practice is to be managed, what is managed must be measured. Meaningful instruments provide measurements that should be compared to the practice's trends and progress, not to national averages. The simplest definition of national average is "The best of the worst or the worst of the best"; quality practices do not wish to be in either position. A caring practice consultant will assist the practice in learning how to use the management instruments available; a dedicated staff will willingly assist in their application.

*To be successful in veterinary practice, the front door must swing
and the phone must ring; that requires clients with animals to be
in your veterinary practice.*
—Logic of the Ages

Population Shifts

In assessing the environment to set the capitalization rate, community demographic trends must be assessed. Children born today are different from those born 30 years ago. Then, only one in four was a first child; now it is nearly one out of every two. People are marrying later in life. In 1960 only 20 percent of mothers even held a part-time job. Today over half are in the paid labor force. These family trends have caused over 25 percent of kids to spend all or part of their day at a nursery school or day-care center. These same trends cause time management to be an important factor in selecting a veterinary practice, especially concerning the density of veterinarians in most urban areas.

Anyone who provides consumer services needs to know that one-third of our total population consists of baby boomers with the peak at 40-something years of age. By age 35, more than 90 percent of the boomers will have been married at least once. The boomers have shown a great interest in health and fitness, committing themselves to taking better care of themselves. Alcohol and tobacco sales have dropped, diet control has increased, and our clients are much more aware of their environments.

Workplace Values

Pre-Boomer 1935-1945	Boomer 1946-1959	Cusper 1960-1965	Buster 1966-1975	Post-TV 1976-1981+
Strong work ethic	Money work ethic	Money/ Principle	Principle/ Satisfaction	To be determined
Hoes to end of row	Usually hoes to end of row	Mixed	Lifestyle first	Lifestyle first
Wants to manage	Wants to manage	Leads and follows	No need to lead	To be determined
Loyal to employer	Loyal to company	Mixed	Loyal to skills	Loyal to skills
Independent but conventional	Cares deeply what others think	Mixed	Doesn't care what others think	Doesn't care what others think
Values working well with others	Wants others to work with him/her	Wants others to work with him/her	Prefers to work alone	Prefers to work alone
Technically savvy	Technically challenged	Technically challenged	Technically savvy	Technically savvy
Follows/honors the leader	Pays lip service to mission	Cares about mission	Must have mission	Must believe in mission
Strong chain of command	Chain of command	Mixed	Individual first	Individual first
Wants to win	Must win	Wants to win	Win/win	Win/win

From 1985 to 1990 the elderly increased about 13 percent, but in the ten years after 1990, the 45-year-plus group grew 46 percent as the baby boomers moved into this age group. During the same 15-year period, the over-85 group also doubled. The need for easier access to facilities, larger print in handouts, and concern for the fixed income of the retired will impact practice growth. Home care services for the elderly will also increase, which will potentially increase the use of house call veterinarians and mobile facilities, since pets are common companions of the house-bound elderly.

Lifestyle Preferences				
Pre-Boomer 1935-1945	**Boomer 1946-1959**	**Cusper 1960-1965**	**Buster 1966-1975**	**Post-TV 1976-1981+**
Works hard, saves money; what is play?	Works hard, plays hard, spends hard	Works hard, plays hard, worries about money	Work hard if it doesn't interfere, saves money	Good grades, makes others pay, saves money
I like it; it's okay	Do you really like it? Will others?	Should I really like it? Will Others?	I like it, I don't care what you think!	Who are you anyway? You're old!
I care about religion	Religion is socially okay	Religion is a hobby	What is religion?	Will I get an "A" in religion?
Exercise is optional	Exercise for body definition	Exercise is a duty	Exercise for mental health	What's your second sport?
Buys a decent home	Buys the most home he/she can	Do I need a house?	Reclaim the inner city	I like living with my parent(s)

Pigeonholed Americans

Birds of a feather flock together, especially if we believe Michael J. Weiss, *The Clustering of America*, (Harper & Row, 1988). Weiss immersed himself in PRIZM, an immense database at Clariotas Corporation in Alexandria, Virginia, and reported on the 250,000 zip code neighborhoods as 40 specific lifestyle groups. If you think you know your average client's profile, you will find the clusters fascinating but frustrating when you see them pigeonholed by Weiss. The real challenge of the PRIZM system is that the analysis was based on the 1980 census (using the SRI classification system called VALS), but the baby boomers diversified during the 1980s into nonspecific groupings that did not fit the VALS profile. The 1990 census data became available and clusters were identified using newer classifications (e.g., the SRI VALS 2).

Social Values

Pre-Boomer 1935-1945	Boomer 1946-1959	Cusper 1960-1965	Buster 1966-1975	Post-TV 1976-1981+
Support United Way	I am forced to support United Way collections	I don't give at the office	United Way isn't "Green"	What is giving?
Red Cross Peace Corps	Battered women's shelter	Homeless shelter	Habitat for Humanity	Greenpeace
Community activities/Rotary	Rotary is good business	Rotary is a bore	What is Rotary and who cares?	Beach sweep, neighborhood clean-up
You must vote	Vote if it is convenient	Vote if you want to	You must vote	To be determined
Quality first, buy American	Prestige first, foreign is better	I'm confused	Cheap, value added	Get it at the Gap

Cluster analysis is a way to group geographic areas by their assumed demographic similarities. The PRIZM system labeled each cluster and rated them by their affluence, from top-ranked "Blue Blood Estates" to bottom-ranked "Public Assistance." It's interesting to note that, based on the 1980 data, the favorite car for the 55-plus age group was the Dodge Diplomat, whether they were "hard scrabble" at $12,874 or "agri-business" at $21,363. If David Letterman is your favorite TV program, you could be in over-55 groups like "two more rungs" or "new melting pot." If *Night Court* and *Cheers* have been your favorite TV passions, you'd fit into the "young suburbia" or "young influentials" cluster. If you drive a Buick Riviera in Ronkonkoma, New York, you fit a "blue-chip blues" profile, while if you drive a Chevy Impala in Butte, Nebraska, you fit the "grain belt" profile. A person who truly belongs in the "new beginnings" cluster is one who drives a Hyundai in San Francisco, California.

Motivation				
Pre-Boomer 1935-1945	**Boomer 1946-1959**	**Cusper 1960-1965**	**Buster 1966-1975**	**Post-TV 1976-1981+**
Money	More money	Do well by doing good	Time off	Time off/out
Responsibility	Promotion	Meeting goals of organization	Meeting own goals	Meeting own wants and goals
Public recognition	Public recognition	Recognition from boss	Recognition from boss	To be determined
Accomplishment	Peer recognition	Bonuses	Skills training	Portable skills training
Desire to lead	Desire for subordinates	Stock options	Stock options	Stock options
Control	Control	Control	Mentoring	Mentoring
Organizational loyalty	Loyalty to self	Loyalty to self	Loyalty to self	Loyalty to self

Weiss observed that the mass market of consumers has been replaced by an ever-expanding list of consumer segments but goes on to ignore it for the sake of the 40 defined segments. Take, for instance, zip code 10019, 65 blocks in New York City. Eighteen were "Single City Blues" (#28), seventeen were "Gray Power" (#13), ten were "Urban Gold Coast" (#4), eight were "Downtown Dixie-Style" (#36), six were "Bohemian Mix" (#11), and six were "New Melting Pot" (#18). In the final analysis, zip code 10019 was classed as "Bohemian Mix" (#11) with no stated reason. If this is the way one zip code breaks down in reality, cluster marketing must be suspect at best. The clusters studied in PRIZM were designed to deliver mail, not to encompass groups of like-minded people. This problem cannot be solved, but it can be avoided.

Communication Styles

Older Workers 1935-1959	Younger Workers 1960-1981+
"We're invincible as a team!"	"I work best alone"
"I want, I think, I would like . . ."	"I need . . ."
Softened style: "I'd love it if you . . ." Long preambles	Blunt style: "Just do it!" Abrupt speech patterns
Good rhetoric and handwriting	Miserable handwriting, uses slang, and "What's rhetoric?"
Likes to process and talk about Ideas, theories, and issues	"Just tell me what you want done, and I will do it!"
Highly value participation and consensus	Do not participate, attend meetings, or need to hear opinions of others
Want people to want to do something; to be part of the group	Want people to get results quickly; often astonished by the feelings or discontent of others
Believes people can be motivated by a stirring, well-expressed idea	Believes motivation is pushing on the end of a rope
Recognition means a great deal; want acceptance, popularity, group identity	Recognition doesn't work and isn't needed; "I know what kind of job I doing. If the boss recognizes my work, that's nice, but it's frosting on the cake."

Alternatives

The census of 1990 offers a far better database to evaluate if you know the definitions of the geographic hierarchy that are used.

- US—the 50 states and the District of Columbia
- Region—Northeast, South, Midwest, and West
- Division—nine groups of states
- State—50, plus D.C.
- County—3,141 counties
- Minor Civil Divisions (MCD) or Census County Divisions (CCD)—29 states have MCD's as county subunits, 21 have bureau-created CCD's
- Place—incorporated or census designated cities, towns, boroughs, and villages that are within a state
- Census Tract/Block Numbering Areas—also county subunits, approximately 4000 people with similar socioeconomic characteristics
- Block Group—subunit of census tract/block numbering area with about 1000 people

• Block—equivalent to a city block, bounded by some physical feature.

Blocks combine to form block groups, which combine to form census tracts, which combine to form counties. The Census Bureau delivers this information to Congress and sells it on laser disk to private industry. Private industry has the responsibility, and freedom, to take the raw data, clean it up, and package it in a way that is useful to business. If you wish to get raw data from the Census Bureau, the annual *Census Catalog and Guide* makes it easy to keep abreast of what is available. You can get a copy of the catalog from the U.S. Government Printing Office, Washington, D.C. 20402, 202-783-3238.

Smart practitioners will realize that they can develop their own target-mailing program from the "cluster" in their medical records. With the release of the 1990 data, all demographic marketing agencies offered a new set of "clusters" upon which to build their recommendations into the next millennium. The new veterinary practice should employ demographic marketing groups like National Decision Systems (Equifax), CACI, NCR, Clariotas, Donnelly, or National Planning Data Corp. for a comprehensive demographic market assessment, and then access a skilled veterinary consultant to interpret the data and develop the potentials of the practice based on the specific catchment area.

Veterinary Healthcare Shift

In addition to community demographic of potential clients, the other veterinary service sources in the community catchment area must be assessed to help establish the risk (capitalization rate). Veterinarians, who last generation treated only sick or injured animals, now offer preventive veterinary care that helps maintain good health and avoid future problems. Clients now have a tendency to anthropomorphize their pets and place similar values on their healthcare needs. Smart veterinarians have shifted from providers to partners in their clients' efforts to maintain the health of their pets.

Boomers, who account for 75 million in our population, are also the most educated generation in history. Twenty years ago only 10 percent of the adults over age 25 had a college degree; today more than 20 percent of them do. Among people in their late 20s, one in four has a degree, and for the first time in history, the men and women of this age group are equal in college education. (Generation X accounts for 45 million of our population.) This information is especially important since women are the primary decision makers in the selection of veterinary healthcare providers.

The most current research, Mediamark 1990, found data that varied from the 1988, 1993, and 1998 demographic reports of the AVMA. Mediamark reported that only 43 percent of U.S. households have pets (AVMA reported over 60 percent). The age of the household affects pet ownership: the 33-44-year-old group showed 56 percent with pets, 45-54 years old reflected 53 percent pet ownership, 44 percent of the 25-34-year-old group had pets, 55-64-years old had a 42 percent pet ownership, and for those over 65 years of age, only 27 percent owned pets. In the suburbs, 46 percent of the homeowners had pets, while of the homeowners in the city, only 39 percent had pets. In cities, 25 percent of the households had dogs while 20 percent of the homes had cats. On the positive side, 57 percent of the couples with kids had pets while only 27 percent of those living alone were pet owners. Mediamark also found that 75 percent of the dog owners and 80 percent of the cat owners bought their pet food in grocery stores. They also reported that $5 billion/year was spent on pets. That amount averages out to $25 per pet per year, if all received equal care, but the data also showed that 78 percent of the dog owners and only 60 percent of the cat owners visited a veterinarian on a regular basis.

Regardless of the demographic data reported by Mediamark, human healthcare research has repeatedly shown that the more educated client wants to be informed about medical procedures, wants to know what alternative treatments are available, and wants to be involved in the medical process. These clients will ask more questions and accept answers they can understand. They want to know why certain conditions exist and what can be done to prevent recurrence. The veterinary practitioner is evaluated today on his or her, or the staff's, client education capabilities. The use of handouts and literature resources is critical and should be customized to the location and practice to appeal to the "new millennium" pet owner.

A FINAL NOTE

Remember these numbers when assessing your own catchment area, since all four numbers should be computed and the lowest estimate used for planning purposes:

✓ Fifty to 60 million dollars of household income is required to support one FTE companion animal veterinarian; mixed and food animal veterinarians must augment this amount with sale barn contract work, production consulting, and other practice-specific variables.

✓ A population of 4000 people, with a 70 percent home dwelling distribution, can generally support one FTE veterinarian.

✓ If 50 percent of the households have pets, and there are 1.6 pets per household, 2300 households are needed to support one FTE veterinarian.

✓ It requires about 1400 returning patients to support one quality-care based companion animal practitioner.

People Sense

Knowing the demographic and psychographic characteristics of your client population is the key to managing today's veterinary practice. It is vital to know the age distribution as well as the financial, occupational, educational, and lifestyle characteristics of the population you expect to serve. This "people sense" is also required in succession planning because as the practice leadership is passed, the followers need to follow.

In every community, demographic characteristics change. For example, a community that has no growth is an aging community; its young people are probably leaving. The aging population is less likely to need evening or weekend practice hours, but they are more likely to desire longer appointments. Seniors tend to exploit any social possibility due to their extra discretionary time.

Growth factor data is simple to obtain. The phone company can give you the number of phone starts and stops in your given prefix area(s) for a specific period of time. The difference is the net growth.

Understanding your clients' occupations is also useful. The engineer-types want data, love the laboratory reports, and will pay for those privileges. Dual-income families will look for evening or weekend hours, as will new families with young children.

The National Center for Health Statistics (NCHS) tabulates human healthcare needs by demographic characteristics. Their inexpensive booklets, which contain incidence rates of most human medical conditions by age, sex, race, and other characteristics, can be useful in estimating both present and future demands within the community. A list of these publications can be obtained by calling NCHS's publications office in Hyattsville, Maryland, at 301-436-8500. While conclusions cannot be blindly imported and applied, community trends can be seen and better understood.

Successful marketing plans use not only demographic but psychographic data as well. "Psychographics" is the new term for describing attitudes, values, and lifestyles. Psychographic information can be obtained through surveys that question how people feel about themselves and about healthcare institutions. SRI of Menlo Park, California, developed "Health VALS"—psychographic information adapted for providers of healthcare. The 1978 VALS system discussed earlier had nine categories and was the only assessment system to really gain wide 1980 census data acceptance. It was organized along a hierarchy of needs, from "survivors" and "sustainers" at the bottom to "integrated" at the top. The three largest groups were "belongers," "achievers," and the "societally conscious." To understand your clients and how they make decisions, you need to understand these groups.

Belongers respond better to messages stressing the old-fashioned values of home, family, and church. Societally conscious people are more likely to respond to messages describing how health services will benefit society. They are also concerned about the environment, have positive feelings toward plants, and tend not to smoke. Achievers are interested in personal success and respond well to fitness and self-care education programs.

For the 1990 census, VALS 2 was unveiled by SRI. SRI believes the link between values, lifestyles, and purchasing choices will become obscured by the aging of the baby boomers, the increasing diversity of the population, and the decline in consumers' expectations for the future. VALS 2 enhances the demographic basics—consumer wants and needs. The demographic evaluation companies that will be using VALS 2 in conjunction with behavior patterns, media usages, and census demographics will have tailored, single-source databases available for specific markets. You can contact *American Demographics* magazine for the best 100 sources for marketing information (800-828-1133).

The Integration Factor of Capitalization Rates

Risk is a factor of the capitalization rate of any valuation formula. When a nationally known veterinary-specific accountant was asked in a seminar, "Why do you use a capitalization rate of five?", his answer was, "Everyone does!" In determining the capitalization rate (degree of risk in recovering the invested money) for this text, demographics, psychographics, average client transaction, community growth trends, and even medical record audits were used. In the hands of its creator, the McCafferty valuation formula is an instrument of perfection; Owen and his team understand this industry and can make the "adjustments" to ensure that the formula "tunes into the practice" and delivers the accurate practice value. In the hands of lesser mortals, the McCafferty formula of *Veterinary Economics* fame (circa 1987) frequently offers only frustration and inaccurate outcomes, yet many practitioners follow it blindly because an accountant created it. The facts here are simple:

- Accountants deal in expenses, usually from your checkbook entries.
- Accountants can talk about expense control with some accuracy.
- Accountants place all income centers into a single pot called revenues (sales, etc.).
- Accountants are targeted at tax law and not at the front door of the practice.
- When income for a line item program or product is compared to the expense associated with that line item, net can be determined; accountants don't do this.

Veterinarians must be aware of the capitalization of clients, their most important practice asset. They must understand the increasing value of the returning client as opposed to the break-even point for the new client. Clinicians also need to understand how people learn their information, or their "media preferences": direct mail, newsletters, newspapers, television, or radio. The simplest fact to remember is that almost all people open their mail. All other media has only a percentage exposure. Multiple, sequential exposures are usually far more successful at causing action than a single exposure. Finally, try to determine *where* the clients in your area go to get veterinary services, *who* is your competition, and *how much* of the total market in your area your practice services.

The valuation formula must have methods to address not only how large or how small your market share is, but also how it changes over time. This involves community demographics, density of veterinary practices in the catchment area, and internal promotion for client bonding. High client loyalty translates into larger market shares. Low market share indicates someone else has developed the client loyalties; a declining market share means something is wrong. When developing your "people sense" marketing plan, the information should answer the following questions:

- Who are the clients?
- What services do they want or need?
- What messages do they respond to best?
- How can they be reached most effectively?
- Where are they currently getting their veterinary services and why?

The answers to these questions help draw a complete picture of today's veterinary care client. Understanding both the detail and overall image of this client portrayal is essential to a successful veterinary practice.

The employment patterns of men and women are converging, putting greater pressure on time and on the necessity to provide alternatives to home care as a client service. The increased demand for high-tech surgery will be accompanied by an expectation for a quick, convenient convalescent period—the fast-food veterinary medicine of the 1990s.

The more highly educated population will place greater value on health maintenance if the focus on patient advocacy has kept them involved in the healthcare process of their pets. Since veterinary healthcare delivery has become a competitive service, the transmission of veterinary medical information to the public will become a critical element of successful practices. This information transmission (e.g., Health Alerts) will be married with target marketing efforts to maximize the effect on potential clients.

Finally, the national trends are merely the sum of the changes that occur in each of our communities. The local trends may vary from the national trends, but they are still vital to the future of any practice. Finding out about your community demographics and using that information to manage your veterinary medical programs will result in better control of the cost of delivering quality care.

"LEG WORK" CAPITALIZATION RATE FACTORS

1. The community demographics (use CACI or Equity Tax sources for up-dated census forecaster).
2. The City/County Planners have a long-term road and community growth plan - get a copy.
3. The "competition" can be other practices, large format pet supply retailers, and even catalog sources, but start with who is in the community:
    a. Plot all practices in the community map if they pull from your "catchment" area.
    b. Assess the degree of the competition: A = super practice, B = clients can't tell the difference, C = shoot & scoot high volume practice, and D = retired in place and dying old practice.
    c. Convert FTE doctors in each practice to "percentage" of pull based on percentage of catchment area overlap and factor in 3b above.
4. The alternatives from "practice coverage voids" appearing in the catchment areas of each practice need to be reviewed for target marketing or practice potentials.

The Appropriate Compensation for Practice Team Members

Leadership is action, not position.

Succession planning is a leadership transition, since the "followers" must also be addressed in the three- to five-year plan. This does not mean cutting salaries to increase net; it means increasing staff leveraging to decrease doctor changes. Therefore, the value of staff must be commensurate with their compensation and needs to be planned at each level. For untrained staff, the process is easy to begin. During the initial orientation phase (non-productive), start them out at slightly above the going rate in your community for starting McDonald's staff; then give them a small raise when they go solo during the introductory employment phase. (Remember, a $0.50 per hour raise costs only $1000 per year.) Concurrently, schedule a wage review and hiring commitment after the introductory period (30 to 90 days, depending on state or province regulations). The hiring decision must always be based on TWO FACTORS: 1) personal competency to the job description provided and 2) the team fit. If either element is lacking at the end of the introductory phase, the practice should cease the relationship. The hiring wage should be established at the end of the introductory phase, based on competency skills and team harmony (also mediated by your community standards and program-based budget). The goal here is to pay these employees the equivalent of your local Sears or J.C. Penney's assistant manager wage by the end of the first year. (These "other employers" are your competitors for staff, and they monitor the community wage scales with a far larger staff than veterinary practices can afford.)

Once a person reaches the first anniversary of employment (he or she is now considered a skilled staff member and warrants business cards with a personalized title of his or her own choosing), compensation should be based on productivity and performance factors, as well as budget planning factors. This varies with each employee. As an example for skilled staff, let's look at the three basic methods to compute the manager's "value to practice" or compensation for performance:

Income Method. Percent of gross (2-4.5 percent). For a savvy administrator, this is often set lower than normally desired during negotiations, and a form of quarterly recognition fees is added to the existing compensation based upon a portion of the excess net (e.g., 20 percent of the increase - OR - 20 percent over the balance sheet requirements).

Market Method. CVPM value (Certified Veterinary Practice Manager by the VHMA), VMI theory course (Veterinary Management Institute by AAHA), college degree(s) (his or her education investment), Diplomate (board certified) of the American College of Healthcare Executives. To wit: What does it cost to buy or raise one of "these" experts?

Cost Method. Compensation required to live within chosen profession, adjusted for costs, amortized equipment (five years), overhead, and taxes to management corporation; charge hours available in year (usually 2500-2600); budget sick, vacation, CE, speaking, etc., to get available hours in annual schedule (usually 1800-2000); division gets hourly fee requirement. But does a single lady cost less to operate than a married guy with three kids?

So looking at the **income-based method**, a two-doctor, $450,000 gross, companion animal practice can afford about 3.0 to 3.5 percent for the manager, or $15,750 (poverty wage even at the high end). But with a quarterly excess net of about $8000, the manager gets an additional $1600 per quarter or about $6400 per year added to the base for an annual compensation of $22,150. This is a reasonable amount, since a two-doctor practice can produce in excess of $700,000-plus in a well-managed operation (which would increase the base to $21,000-plus starting from the conservative end).

For the **market method**, you would negotiate the worth of experience and knowledge, and if necessary, obtain the VHMA annual salary survey data for your region (but you may not like being "average").

When using the **costing method**, let's start with the following example: $30,000 compensation + $5000 benefit costs + $15,000 facility overhead expenses + $10,000 taxes (payroll, etc.) = $60,000, divided by 2000 available hours means $30/hour should be the break-even rate to be assessed.

The bottom line, as a veterinary practice consultant, is that no one in a leadership role should hold out for a hefty *base* salary. A real healthcare administrator and practice leader will need to be ready to receive the rewards of practice success and the anguish of practice failure. I use the term "leader" because that is what these turbulent times require. The easiest method to differentiate a leader from a manager is to watch their management style. A leader will use situational leadership, since they realize their job is to accomplish the mission (task) through other people. A manager will have programs and projects and will dwell on "following the book" for self and others.

Another good definition is, *"A leader gives credit and takes blame while a manager takes credit and gives blame."* A caring leader realizes that the team is the strength and the process is the limitation; the outcome is what really counts. A progressive leader has confidence in the team and shares the rewards, gives the recognition, and nurtures each individual as a special practice asset. A leader also shares accountability for outcomes. A traditional veterinary manager controls expenses, establishes policy and procedures, and assigns jobs (tasks) as needed.

Managers who desire a hefty base pay are not potential leaders; they want a guarantee regardless of performance. This is a warning flag. Practices should pay for performance, not promises. True leaders trust in their people and the capabilities of the team to make improvements, solve problems, and increase client services (and thus increase the liquidity). A healthcare administrator will ask for a percentage of success and then ask the team to excel. He or she will establish expectations, offer individualized training, and nurture the development of others as program managers to enable the practice to reach those objectives.

Leadership is evidenced at every workstation or in every process stream. The recognition of this skill in all staff is the first evidence of wisdom in the senior leadership. To allow colleagues to acquire increased responsibility is to potentiate the very best in each of the people you work with and build that bond that will endure. **Developing others is the beginning of meaningful succession planning.** Remember, managers get work done through people while leaders develop people through work. Even veterinarians can learn to lead!

Let the Doctors Earn What They Are Worth

Time to earn your paycheck!

In effective succession planning, you do not "pay" people to buy-in, but as they buy-in, they deserve competitive compensation for work, ROI, and division of excess net. This is an important factor to consider when setting the stage for "the next level." A few parameters must be understood here. The schools have taken to setting the salary expectations of the graduating veterinarians, and some schools have even begun brokering their graduates between practices. This is very interesting coming from institutions that cannot operate at a profit, have very little "real world" client experience, and cannot produce a primary care veterinarian. The new graduates are great at tertiary care, but when it comes to client relations, staff interaction, and common healthcare delivery requirements, they are not yet trained veterinarians.

The preferred method of compensating employed veterinarians in the industry appears to be similar to the methods used to set the paraprofessional staff salaries: get the labor for as little as possible and then ask for 110 percent commitment by the individual. I don't know why we do it to ourselves, but it seems to be the rule, not the exception. The July 1990 *Veterinary Economics* article, "Compensation Tactics: New Alternatives," provided some insight into what was common in the marketplace as we entered the 1990s. The subsequent issues each fall, with their economic surveys, have steadily gone downhill. I personally believe the reports were victims of statistical inaccuracies rather than national trends. But then, after visiting about 1200 veterinary hospitals, my perspectives are probably a bit slanted. We visit only the hospitals that want to change and do better; status quo practices do not ask to be certified by AAHA nor do they request consultations by leadership-based firms like ours. This concept is meant to spark your interest in catching up with the trends of tomorrow rather than in keeping up with the trends of yesterday.

The New Graduate

The 1999 new graduate expected to earn $40,000 a year or more and to commit 40 hours or less per week to a veterinary practice. This expectation usually precludes emergency call and overtime concerns and includes a minimum of two days off each week. For the record, we recommend to our clients that they accept this expectation as reality, since the new graduate does. But that does not mean the salary guarantee must continue past the first year or that pay increases will come by tenure. Read on please!

Most veterinary schools will no longer give out details about the new graduates. Rather, they will verify that graduation occurred on a specific date and that the graduate was in good standing. The salary offered varies by community, not by school of graduation. The new graduate is likely to generate a gross of only $80,000 to $150,000 the first year, dependent on practice philosophy, scope of services, and client/patient mix, as well as personal ability and confidence; by the end of the second year, however, these numbers should double, within the limitations of similar parameters. Since most practices realize only a 15 to 30 percent net profit, the new graduate should expect only about 20 percent of the gross personally generated, plus benefits. Starting salaries in most areas of the country average from $36,000 to $48,000, depending on benefits. A performance pay for production in excess of $16,000 per month (say 7 percent of anything over that target dollar amount) can be offered, as can a premium for taking emergency calls (e.g., keeping all the emergency fee plus a percentage of the remaining ticket). If you really want to have fun, get involved in the junior externship programs from the surrounding veterinary schools, and if the students you meet there have the personality you like (remember, we hire for attitude, then train to competency), do something about it! Offer them a senior-year scholarship. Yes, offer significant money as a scholarship, in a contractual exchange for a work commitment of one year at the going rate. This is not only a substantial tax deduction, but it also gives both the future associate and the practice a feeling of future security.

We also tell our practice-owning clients to expect to subsidize the new graduate for six months and not to expect them to be net producers during that time. New graduates learned tertiary care at the knees of academic experts who too often state, "*... you can't afford to do this in practice, but we will do it here ...*"; they can transplant kidneys but can't do a dental or treat a cat fight abscess. We recommend new graduates be given an extra ten minutes per client per appointment for three months, with the expectation that they will come into alignment with the practice philosophy before six months of tenure. They decide when to revert to the expectation, between three and six months of employment, because at six months, productivity pay should start. The practice should be ready to pay at least $1400 twice a month for six months, without concern, and then shift to a percentage of production for increased compensation beyond starting base. In true team-based practices, the doctors are paid on practice productivity rather than personal productivity, because the leader has removed the "I" and "me" pronouns from his or her vocabulary and replaced them with "we" and "us" concepts. The ownership needs to be prepared to pay more when the doctor earns more than the guaranteed base, and to pay it with a smile and a song in their hearts.

PREFERRED PRODUCTION METHOD

- The base pay will be 19 to 20 percent of the previous year's personal production, divided over 24 pay periods (never to be debated again).
- The production pay is based on a practice-set goal each month and divided among the team by a specific formula tailored to the practice.
- Increases in base pay percentages (0.5 percent increments) are only given when the person assumes practice support functions (e.g., in-service training) that takes them away from clients and patients.

How long has it been since you tore up roots and moved to a new area? Massive costs are involved in just getting there. Piled on top of student loans, repairs on the old car, and outfitting the crowd for life off-campus, the up-front cost of moving may be outside the budget of a good candidate. Consider indentured servitude: offer to pay the costs of moving. In return for this courtesy, the candidate will less likely bolt and run after one year. During the first year, each month's work will "pay off" (forgive) 1/12th of the moving/shipping costs. If the candidate runs early, he or she will owe the practice the unredeemed portion of the moving bill. This is an up-front benefit that will appear very generous to a candidate (it is) and start your relationship on a good footing. The candidate knows this is candy because he or she is sure he or she is good for *at least* one year and is willing to commit to the mutually caring relationship.

"What gets measured, gets managed!"

The formula offered in Example 1 of Appendix B is based on critical elements of performance, which include client perceptions, staff perceptions, community perceptions, ownership perceptions, and fiscal success of the practice. This concept changes the associate's perspective from the bottom line to the front door. It changes the associate's level of team interaction as well and the diversity of his/her personal life. The criteria mix could easily be changed, based on the practice philosophy and direction (Example 2, Appendix B). In mixed practice or food animal practice, the criteria would likely include the different elements of the practice (e.g., sale barn satisfaction versus producer feedback). Let us first look at the sample criteria for a progressive veterinary practice:

1. Since every practice wants to improve patient-client service, clients need to be asked about their perceptions. A quarterly survey on the quality of service would provide client feedback about each provider, as well as the practice system that supports the client access. The results of the survey would then set the criteria for the next three months.

2. The individual veterinarian's active involvement in community activities is important to the practice and to the veterinarian's own quality of life. Here we have both succession planning and leadership in action! The community activity should be of the veterinarian's own choosing and be one that promotes community image, health, and/or wellness, as well as the veterinarian's identity to community members.

3. Most practices are also concerned with the veterinarian's timely and satisfactory performance of all administrative and non-patient care responsibilities. This could be as simple as a dress code or as complex as the training of outpatient nurses. These succession plan and delegation development efforts include both one-time tasks and recurring accountabilities which may be assigned from time to time by the practice leadership or assumed by the

team members of a well-functioning healthcare delivery team.

4. Since staff produces net and doctors produce only the gross, an evaluation of each doctor by the paraprofessional team is important, addressing harmony, synergy, and quality of practice performance. This would be in the form of a simple survey done quarterly to establish the criteria for the next three months (also applicable to Example #2). Team members should be able to help develop and define team standards, and this category provides a mechanism that helps this endeavor.

5. Regardless of the individual effort, a program-based budget sets goals and objectives for the programs being offered by the specific practice. The entire practice should be working to attain or exceed the financial projections for these programs. Practice projections should provide for a total annual growth of at least the inflation rate (Consumer Price Index minus CPI) plus 6 percent (projected need to support a benefit plan investment program, debt retirement, and capital expense procurement needs).

6. Each business unit is assessed for team member participation. While the clinical aspects initially appear limited and elements like sale barn, boarding facility, grooming operations, resale boutique and brood mare farms appear specific, staff overlaps are actually the area for succession planning development.

   - What can a skilled nursing staff member actually do?
   - Where can animal caretakers become nursing staff extenders?
   - Can the paraprofessional staff become owners in ancillary areas?
   - Is "ownership" in operational accountability linked to fiscal ownership?
   - How are tenured staff members utilized to develop a succession in interest?

The Second-Year Veterinarian

A second-year veterinarian is a healthcare professional with a track record that can be verified and one who knows what they are capable of producing in a given practice situation. While a salary addition of $4000 to $5000 is about average for each year of employment (up to six years), this is the time that a productivity percentage should be offered in lieu of salary. The development of a program-based budget (Chapter 4, *Building The Successful Veterinary Practice: Programs &*

Procedures (Volume 2), published by ISUP) should make the ownership aware that whether it be a base salary, productivity compensation, or a combination of the two, the bottom line is always **the compensation packages are a percentage of gross income.** Twenty percent of the previous year's production is a good starting point for doctor negotiations. Percentages higher than 20 percent should include a reciprocal reduction of the benefit package.

The Experienced Veterinarian

Because a quality practitioner should be able to produce a gross of $250,000 to $450,000 per year, a straight percentage increase will usually have a ceiling. Salaries for general practitioners should also hit a ceiling at about $65,000 to $75,000, depending on the local cost of living. In certain areas of the country (e.g., Southern California or the Northeast), the minimum earnings need to exceed $350,000, and the salary base is equally inflated. In high-density scheduling and other veterinary extender programs, doubling this income production ceiling is possible, but that is a topic for another time. After this level of salaried or percentage income, multiple methods of profit sharing become the key ways to increase personal liquidity for an individual veterinarian.

Bonus Plans

The term "bonus" denotes a gift. But in veterinary practice, every dollar is earned. We use the term "recognition pay" to ensure that owners and staff remember that performance comes before remuneration. Our salaried team members expect appropriate levels of personal income, and practice owners must create the environment for success. In the next millennium, this decade's innovation will become commonplace. This includes the inventory management team being paid 20 percent of savings below 13 percent cost of goods sold; the receptionist being rewarded by setting the critical performance point at 80 percent appointment log fill, then giving him/her 20 percent of all income over that target point; the nutritional counselors sharing 20 percent of the nutritional product sales growth over a programmed growth rate (e.g., 10 percent); the behavior counselors getting 20 percent of their time charges; and even the hospital managers earning 10-20 percent of the excess net (after balance sheet monies) per quarter. Other "benefits" for professionals include sabbaticals and extended continuing education experiences, as well as profit-sharing, retained earnings programs, and flexible spending accounts. Do not overlook acquiring the "right" to nominate the next capital expense budget "toy" for the practice acquisition list as a benefit of professional involvement in practice success.

New Pay Plans

We are at a revolution in reward systems - it's not something that is going to go away.
—Rob Heneman, Ohio State University

The days of tenure and consumer price index raises are coming to a close, and the era of compensation for performance is emerging. Finally alternatives that can be applied to veterinary medicine without a degree in business or a complex computer formula (examples #1 & #2 above) will be tested and talked about. Maybe it is just because these alternatives are starting to mimic some of the programs we have found successful in our consulting efforts, but we like this trend! Here is the current terminology applied to these ideas:

Gainsharing (also called Team-Based Pay). For every dollar the practice exceeds its goal(s), 20 percent is shared with staff. This includes the premise that the practice has pre-established goals that the staff can affect. Gainsharing is a monthly or quarterly system that targets specific programs or specific line item financial goals, rather than the overall profitability of the practice.

Broadbanding. Broadbanding allows individuals to be recognized for their contributions without a "promotion" into another level of the business. The goal here is to allow increased pay for increased responsibility.

Lump-Sum Merit Pay. Come raise time, the business gives one large check, rather than spreading a small raise over the full year. While this is great for investment tools like the simple and Roth IRAs, the bad news is that the salary base does not change.

Competency-Based Pay. This takes more planning and better training standards than most practices currently use. This is what we use during the orientation and probationary periods of new hires, but competency-based pay can be applied to income center development efforts too.

"At Risk" Pay. "At risk" pay is usually measured by an outside benchmarking firm. If the goals are met, the salaried manager gets the money, but if the goals are missed, the money stays with the company. The pay system is therefore directly linked to the corporate vision.

Professional Motivation

Professional motivation is that inner drive that causes us to want to make better diagnostic judgments or to develop more effective treatment plans. Professional motivation is the pride taken in relieving suffering or helping a client through a tough pet illness. It has nothing to do with internal marketing, personnel management, time effectiveness, cost efficiency, or other routine practice management concerns. It is not restricted to the DVM Clan nor is it automatically conferred with the academic degree. (Actually, the more educated people are, the less diversity we usually see in their daily lives.)

Cooperative Practice Progression

To get owner, employed veterinarian, and staff going in the same direction as the practice requires certain basic actions:

1. In a quiet and unhurried time, make a genuine veterinarian-to-staff-to-veterinarian effort to share the practice philosophy as well as its business goals and objectives.
2. Ensure that everyone understands that the team effort toward practice goals and objectives takes precedent over individual bias and whims.
3. Develop measurements for progress that can be determined, and reward the achievements with accolades (and possibly a bonus if profit is involved).

The long-term progression toward a practice goal will probably involve a greater commitment and more cooperation than described in the three steps above, especially if the senior owner wants to reduce his/her personal hours at the facility. This type of situation will require more innovation ... maybe after the first 18 months of employment, the bonus monies will be stopped or capped, but a schedule for equity rewards becomes available. The rewards don't have to be enormous, maybe only a 1 to 2 percent share each year that the net increases. Under the current tax laws, offering an employed veterinarian a 1 to 2 percent share each year in which the practice net improves is an easy way to transfer property without a major tax hike in capital gains. It also demonstrates a long-term commitment and shares the return on investment (ROI) with the employee, which eases the pay-off hit. Another similar concept involves paying the practice manager a percentage of the net (gross income less total monthly expenses) that is over the expected monthly ROI (Return On Investment) of the practice.

Hot Buttons

The real secret to motivating any employee is to find the "hot button"— that idea or wish that excites the heart and mind of the employee. Play to that need. If the veterinarian believes surgery skills could be improved, find a special course, maybe even an orthopedic course in Switzerland, and build toward that goal for six to eight months. Other practice goals may not be reached that easily. If *you* want the veterinarian to sell more dog food, you may need to rethink *your* plan; nutritional counseling is staff country! Maybe all you need is to get more internal referrals from the veterinarian to one of your technicians who really believes in quality diets. It is easier to redefine the problem than try and solve one that doesn't actually exist.

Hot buttons may be owner commitment to the associate veterinarian, to staff development, or to the future of the practice itself. It is critical that the future be identifiable, especially if the veterinarian or staff member is trying to support a family. Is there a real commitment to providing quality time for the veterinarian or staff member to pursue outside interests like a family or even hobbies? The appropriate "hot buttons" for each veterinarian or paraprofessional on the staff vary, and some have many, others only one. The secret to motivation is a leader's skill in finding that "special" element of personal well-being for each team member, creating the environment that allows it to be developed, and then playing to the specific "hot buttons" during professional development efforts.

Putting It All Together

It must be reiterated that compensation is only one recognition method. In most healthcare worker surveys, money was among the top six motivators, but it never made it to number one in ANY staff survey. The compensation/motivation key, of course, is that any decisions made relating to personal behavior must be voluntary. The need for change may be pointed out by someone else, but the target person must genuinely accept it if any permanent change is to be accomplished. The most striking and long-lasting changes in personality or performance are those that the individual recognizes as important to his or her own personal growth.

There are some typical actions that most successful managers use to encourage employees to improve their performance. They try to:

✓ Avoid passing on anxieties, emotions, and doubts to the staff.
✓ Criticize without being damning, hostile, or cynical.
✓ Be sensitive to the needs of their staff without appearing to be paternal.
✓ Be forceful without being domineering.
✓ Disagree without being offensive.
✓ Compliment people without exaggerating.
✓ Build on strength, encouraging all that is positive.

Part of establishing firm objectives and measurements with any employee is jointly determining how changes will be advantageous. Nothing helps your staff over the hurdles like a clear reminder that there is a monetary recognition benefit that can result. Getting feedback from others on changes is the best way to gauge the results of your efforts. Review the Evaluation Leadership Skill, Appendix B in Volume 1, *Building the Successful Veterinary Practice: Leadership Tools*, published by ISUP, then answer these questions:

• Is improvement taking place?
• If not, why not?
• If so, to what extent?
• What remains to be done?
• Have I done all I can do to help my staff achieve the change(s)?

Especially at first, the feedback a leader receives is likely to be unpleasant. It might even be painful. Being able to take criticism is a sign of a leader's managerial strength. Only by accepting the unflattering comments can a leader improve the perceived deficiencies; only by addressing the perceptions can a leader gain the confidence and trust of the staff team in their worth. The team environment and peer pressure will motivate its members.

Benefit Programs for Staff

"In economics, the majority is usually wrong!"

The above pithy grabber was provided during my pursuit of a Masters in Healthcare Administration at Baylor University. The author was unknown, but almost all the experienced managers in the room realized the rational basis of the statement. Physicians are paid based on the labor of the paraprofessionals who support their patients, and the paraprofessionals get what is left. I prefer to use the term "paraprofessionals" because "lay staff" or "employees" does not describe most of the dedicated people who serve the healthcare professions in America today. In my opinion, this concept of paraprofessionals equally applies to the majority of the 1200-plus veterinary practices I've visited since 1987.

The Color of Money

I have consulted one practice where the paraprofessional staff were paid only 12 percent of the gross and were overpaid, while at another practice the staff compensation budget was 26 percent of the gross and it was rational. Other practices are distributed throughout that range. What is "normal" for the average practice requires the "average" to be quantified, and that has yet to occur in our profession. Every veterinary practice utilizes its staff differently, and in many cases, under-utilizes them differently as well.

Some practices have started to award continuing education days based on tenure: the more years, the more need to learn new things. The days might be paid as eight-hour workdays but a stipend (per diem) is always provided for registration, lodging, and meals associated with the meeting. The per diem amount varies with a set of variables associated with the productivity of the practice. When continuing education is funded by the practice, there is one requirement: bring at least one idea home per day of subsidized continuing education and unilaterally (practice has NO veto power) be responsible for implementing the idea(s). This is called "trusting the staff," and it is outside the comfort zone of some large but stagnating practices; see the cause and effect? After 90 days of implementation, the leadership team should conduct an evaluation of the program(s) for the cost-benefit factors (to the client, to the staff, and/or to the net).

Another system involves the veterinary receptionist, animal caretaker, and technician teams holding a practice together; they have the majority of client and patient contact time. If I could be king for a day, I would mandate an incremental wage increase package during the first year of training that would reach the level commensurate with acquired responsibility (remember the Sears and J.C. Penney formulas). After the first year, as discussed earlier, all increases would be based on productivity improvements of the individual and/or the practice. Receptionist productivity could be linked to appointment log fill rates or new client referral rates. Technician nurses could have productivity interests in nutritional counseling, behavior management, dental hygiene activities, and related special interests. Animal caretakers could have their productivity linked to baths, playtime, total practice growth, or in-house efficiencies. Employed veterinarians are already on production-based income. All these production compensation concepts require owner supervision of stated performance EXPECTATIONS.

Other systems have been implemented with some success, but most of them require that an annual cash budget be available for the practice. You see, we have started to pay on saved money or excess income; this is called "sharing the net." It is unwise to put the staff on a share of gross income unless a cash budget is in effect. One of the more fun methods we have started to use of late with practices that care where they are relative to a cash budget involves recognizing staff salary savings. The concept is simple. Consider that the lead receptionist assumes accountability for keeping the reception staff payroll dollars below the cash budget. If the cash budget goal for receptionists is 6 percent of gross quarterly, the lead receptionist would receive 10 percent of the savings under 6 percent as a management fee, the receptionist staff divides shares of an additional 30 percent, and the owners put 30 percent away for the pre-Christmas productivity award (ownership keeps the balance for tax purposes as well as their budget concerns). At the end of the year, the receptionist salary comes in under budget! In the best of all possible worlds, tenure would NEVER be a reason for "merit pay" increases.

Appendix A shares computation and valuation formats of fiscal self-assessment that can lead to a complex financial planning problem. To use only your own resources to solve the investment picture is silly. You have bankers, brokers, accountants, and financial planners on your client list whom you trust and who will work for your benefit with their expertise. Cultivate the resources available to you, and program your financial future as you would your practice growth. Know exactly where you want to be next year, in three years, and in five years from a practice perspective and a financial goal system. If you don't know when or where you want to retire, set some general business and practice goals to help establish the retirement or resale potential that could be measured and evaluated within the one-three-five-year goal setting program.

Selecting the Right Future

Every decision carries a consequence!
—A fact of life

The experience of Catanzaro and Associates points to one inestimable action an owner can take to maintain practice value. Most single practitioners expect to find a "feller," when the time is right to be a "seller." Most practitioners don't plan for when the time is right to sell.

The old valuation system of taking the annualized average of three years gross as the practice price is valid ONLY if: 1) 20 percent net growth has occurred annually, 2) there is no debt, AND 3) someone is willing to buy it at that price (a rare combination in today's buyer market). The "70-80 percent of gross" thumb rule is becoming a closer approximation of the average companion animal practice. Specialty practices and production livestock practices have a value in real assets, but little else; reputations carry these practices. Therefore, some form of partnership and/or shared ownership is essential for increasing their value at retirement.

The transition of ownership, and practice leadership must be initiated a full business cycle before the anticipated retirement date, since the practice's leadership should be transferred smoothly for the purpose of staff and client retention. This often requires a mediator (a qualified consultant and mentor) to assist all parties and maintain harmony and practice pride. (**Quality is what the clients call pride.**)

If you are a young practitioner, start banking/investing 10 percent of your take-home every month, effectively immediately with NO excuses. Also, at the end of every year, whether you are a practice owner or a productivity-based associate getting an end-of-year bonus, place 50 percent of the excess net into solid real estate investments in your own community. In this manner, practice sale becomes supplemental money, not primary retirement income.

As we said at the end of Chapter One, these points are made simply because too many practices fail to plan ahead, and **the public veterinary corporations are NOT always the answer.** If you cannot see your practice days ending, or you see only one method of exit, then succession planning is even more critical. Succession planning is how to move from one point of your veterinary medical evolution to the next level of life. It needs to be done today and committed to completely, regardless of the evolutionary point you are at, since life and family are forever, and practice is just transitory. Today is already yesterday's tomorrow, and nothing stopped it from happening: learn from that fact. Plan for the future, and it won't be scary.

CAPITALIZATION RATE SUMMARY

1. Dead practice worth tangible assets only
2. A shrinking practice with negative growth (NO NET, DECREASING CLIENTS, DECREASING SERVICES) and no tenured staff
3. A shrinking practice, in client, growth services, +/- high turnover of key staff
4. Average mature practice in static community with growth in net just above CPI and staff "doing what they are told"
5. Average practice in average community with at least two times CPI growth in net (after equitable salaries, appropriate ROI, and reasonable capital expenses)
6. Growing practice in average community with at least three times CPI growth in pure net
7. Growing practice in growing community with at least three times CPI growth in pure net and trained staff
8. Growing mature practice in rapidly expanding community, net growth above 15 percent pure net after balance sheet monies, and interactive healthcare team; no competition in catchment area
9. Growing mature practice in rapidly expanding community, net growth above 15 percent pure net after balance sheet monies, and interactive healthcare team; no competition in catchment area, plus new facility without liabilities, plus tax break incentives from the community

---

Legal Issues of Veterinary Practice Succession Plans

3

Chapters 1 and 2 examined succession planning in the context of the alternatives available to a veterinary practice owner to accomplish his or her goals through effective practice management and planning. The remaining chapters focus on succession planning from a legal point of view. Chapter 3 defines succession planning from a legal perspective and examines the legal and economic goals and options available to a veterinary practice.

What is a veterinary practice succession plan?

The concept of veterinary succession plans is foreign to many veterinarians. A veterinary succession plan is not a financial retirement plan, although there are important financial implications to a succession plan. It is not a tax plan, although there are important tax consequences to a veterinary practice succession plan. A veterinary practice succession plan is a plan of action to enable an owner to exit his or her practice at a time of his or her choosing and to maximize the after-tax profits from the sale. It can be very detailed if the veterinarian wants to implement the plan in the near future, or it can be very general if the veterinarian is not acting on the plan for many years.

What are the four legal/economic benefits to creating a veterinary practice succession plan?

1. **Forces Veterinarian to Plan Long-Term for Practice.**

   A veterinarian's ownership interest in his or her practice is often his or her most valuable asset and is frequently a major source of retirement income. The planning involved in the selling of such a valuable and important asset needs to be addressed with the same level of attention and detail as is given to a retirement plan or a child's education fund. A veterinary practice succession plan forces a veterinarian to direct his or her attention and energies to making long-term planning decisions.

2. **Expands Options to Minimize Risk.**

   The primary goal of a veterinary practice succession plan is to permit an owner of a veterinary practice to exit his or her practice when he or she wants and to maximize his or her after-tax profits. In this regard, a veterinarian who is planning a succession plan will commonly consult with his or her advisers and obtain advice regarding the best type of transaction to meet these goals. The veterinarian may be advised that the best scenario for his or her situation is to have a buyer pay the asking price in cash when the veterinarian is ready to retire. Unfortunately, the best-case scenario goals are difficult to realize.

   It is very important that a selling veterinarian be flexible and willing to consider all of his or her succession planning options in order to minimize the risks associated with these types of transactions. A selling veterinarian needs to understand that there is more than one structure that can be utilized to meet his or her goals. It is a very risky decision for a veterinarian to decide that there is only one way to accomplish his or her goals. An example is a selling veterinarian who has decided that the only succession planning structure that he or she is comfortable accepting is the cash purchase of his or her assets. All too frequently, buyers with the financial ability to purchase the practice do not appear when the seller is ready to sell. When this happens the selling veterinarian is forced to continue practicing after he or she wanted to retire or is forced to hire an associate to operate the practice after the selling veterinarian retires. This is risky for the selling veterinarian because the market value will be reduced if the practice does not maintain a certain level of production. It is also a reality that certain buyers fail to comply with the terms of their agreements when the seller accepts a promissory note as part of the purchase price. When this happens, a selling veterinarian will normally be forced to take back the practice and operate it until he or she can find another buyer. This may not be a problem if the seller is 60 years old and is in good health, but it can be a big problem to a seller who is 65 and in bad health. In this situation also, the seller may be forced to hire an associate to operate the practice until the seller finds another buyer. Unfortunately, the transition between veterinarians will usually result in a substantial decline in practice revenues and value.

The reality for most selling veterinarians is that they will be unable to find a buyer who can obtain financing to pay the seller the full purchase price at closing. This may not be ideal because of the risk; however, it is a reality for most sellers. The seller needs to accept this fact and explore alternatives available in order to maximize his or her comfort level in the transaction.

3. Maximizes After-Tax Value of Veterinary Practice.

Veterinarians frequently fail to focus on the bottom line profitability of their practice, which affects the after-tax value of the practice. All too frequently veterinarians fail to balance providing affordable care to owners of animals with the priority of having a productive and profitable practice.

We have found that one of the reasons veterinarians are opposed to creating succession plans is that they do not believe that their practice has much value. We have been involved in transactions where veterinarians in multiple-doctor practices have contractually obligated themselves to sell their interest for a below market value regardless of their ability to sell for fair market value on the open market. We have also been involved in transactions where selling veterinarians are interested in selling their practices to associate veterinarians in small percentages over a ten-year period of time without requiring the value of the interest to be periodically updated. A selling veterinarian who agrees to either of these structures is losing the increase in value resulting from his or her efforts to promote and develop the practice.

Careful planning of the structure of a succession plan can have significant after-tax effects upon the value of the selling veterinarian's practice. In order to accomplish their goals, veterinarians must examine their succession plan options with enough time to implement. Many options available to maximize the after-tax benefit cannot be implemented on a short-term basis.

4. Creates a Market for Your Practice.

A thoroughly analyzed veterinary practice succession plan can expand the number of potential buyers and create a market that the selling veterinarian had not previously considered. Frequently, veterinarians fail to create succession plans because they are confident that they will find viable buyers for their practices. Many veterinarians believe that a large public or private corporation will be in the market to buy their practices when they decide to retire. Unfortunately, when they begin marketing their practices, many selling veterinarians discover that there are few large corporations that are actively acquiring veterinary practices.

Selling veterinarians who believe they will not have any trouble finding a qualified (non-corporate) buyer do not realize that the majority of individual veterinarians wanting to acquire a practice do not have the liquidity for a substantial down payment. They frequently expect the seller to carry 90 percent or more of the selling price. This problem is further compounded in that traditional lenders are hesitant to loan money to veterinarians to purchase practices without the buyer pledging collateral above and beyond his or her ownership interest in the veterinary practice being purchased.

There are of course exceptions. Some corporations, for example, are purchasing veterinary practices to break into certain geographic markets or to increase their market share in certain areas. In addition, we have dealt with many transactions where parents of young veterinarians either personally guarantee the loan of a buying veterinarian or simply purchase the practice for their child. However, like the large corporate acquisition, this is unusual relative to the total number of practice transactions that occurs every year.

While a selling veterinarian may be lucky enough to have a large corporation purchase his or her practice or to find a buyer with adequate collateral to borrow money for purchasing a practice, it could be devastating to plan only for the most optimistic of transition strategies.

When should you create a veterinary practice succession plan?

It is important for a selling veterinarian to explore his or her succession plan options years before the target date for exiting the practice in order to maximize his or her options. It is not unusual for an associate buy-in structure to take up to ten years to complete. A selling veterinarian who waits until two years before his or her target date to separate from the practice has minimized his or her options in structuring a succession plan transaction.

It is never too early to begin succession planning, in that it is impossible to predict when a veterinarian will need to exit his or her practice. This point is clearly demonstrated by a scenario that frequently arises when veterinarians are unable to continue to practice as a result of health problems. An unexpected forced exit from a practice due to health concerns may be problematic for veterinarians who have succession plans, but it will definitely be financial disaster for a veterinarian who has not created a succession plan.

A selling veterinarian without an implemented succession plan who is forced to exit the practice for health reasons is frequently a motivated seller. If the seller cannot work at all, he or she will have hired an associate or a relief veterinarian to maintain the practice's production. Unfortunately, this typically results in a reduction in the practice's production and a corresponding reduction in the value of the practice. A selling veterinarian in this situation frequently needs to maximize the after-tax net income from the practice to replace the income that he/she and his/her family have been accustomed to receiving. The selling veterinarian will also want a buyer who will pay most if not all of the purchase price at closing.

A veterinarian who finds him- or herself in this situation is unlikely to quickly find a buyer who can come up with the cash. If the veterinarian does have a cash offer for purchase, he or she is at risk of the potential buyer realizing his or her leverage in this situation and demanding a significant purchase price discount. The likelihood is that, absent good fortune, the veterinarian will be forced to sell to a buying veterinarian who will require that the seller finance the bulk of the purchase price over a five- to ten-year period.

A seller who is forced to accept payments on an installment sale of his or her practice has greatly increased the risk involved. A certain amount of risk is always involved for a selling veterinarian who is forced to accept payments over time. However, this risk is dramatically increased if the selling veterinarian would not be physically able to resume operating the practice should the buyer fail to make the payments.

The level of risk is much less for a veterinarian who has structured a stair-step buy-in for an associate as his or her succession plan. This veterinarian will most likely have a stockholders agreement that requires the associate to buy the seller's remaining ownership interest in the practice in the event that the veterinarian is unable to work because of health reasons. The buyer and seller might have purchased disability insurance to fund the buy-out of the remaining ownership interest of the seller.

NEED FOR SUCCESSION PLANNING

Pros: • Expands your options
       • Reduces your risks associated with the transaction

Cons: • May be ineffective because the future cannot be predicted with accuracy

---

What are your options in structuring a veterinary succession plan transaction?

A multitude of options are available when structuring a veterinary succession plan transaction. The choice of transaction structure will vary dramatically depending upon whether the buyer is buying all or part of the practice. A buyer who is either buying all of the stock in a corporation or all of the assets of the practice will have a structure that is substantially different from a buyer who is buying a percentage of an existing practice. There are, however, a few basic transaction structures that encompass almost all succession plan transactions. The transaction will ordinarily fall into one or two general categories: asset sale or stock sale. There are some basic distinctions between the two types of sale transactions that are important for a selling or a buying veterinarian to understand:

Asset Sale Structure

A veterinary practice asset sale is almost always used when one or more buyers are acquiring an entire existing practice. The buyer will have formed his or her own business entity for taking title and operating the practice. If there are multiple buyers, they, as part of their business structure, will have adopted agreements between them to control the buy-out of each other's interest in the event of the death, disability or retirement of one or more of the buyers. These agreements, however, will not involve the selling veterinarian.

In a veterinary practice asset sale, the buyer has the opportunity to pick and choose which assets he or she wants to purchase from the seller. There are certain assets that selling veterinarians will commonly exclude or sell through a separate transaction. These types of assets include accounts receivable, cash on hand, bank accounts, company automobiles, and personal items of the selling veterinarian, i.e. books, art, etc.

Another aspect of an asset sale is that the buying veterinarian can select which liabilities of the selling veterinarian he or she is willing to assume by taking over the responsibility to pay. An example of this is a service contract on a software program that the seller has contracted to receive. The buyer may not be interested in using the current system and might refuse to assume the service contract obligation. This can frequently be a substantial issue for the selling veterinarian who will want all practice liabilities to be assumed, regardless of the buyer's desires.

There are also certain tax issues present with an asset sale that do not apply to certain stock sales. Sellers of assets will normally be required to pay taxes on the recapture of tax depreciation that had previously been taken on the acquisition of hard assets of the practice, i.e., chairs, desks, computers. The amount of the recapture of the depreciation tax deduction will be based upon an allocation of the purchase price between the categories of assets being sold. If there is gain beyond the original acquisition cost of the hard assets of a company, that gain will be taxed at a capital gain rate. This is a rarity, however, because most hard assets will lose their value over time.

Buyers of assets need to be aware that the tax allocation agreement that identifies the purchase price for each type of asset being sold will control the length of time the buyer is permitted to depreciate the purchase price as a tax deduction. In 1993, the Internal Revenue Code was amended to permit buyers of assets to depreciate goodwill of a practice over 15 years. Prior to this amendment, a buyer was not permitted to amortize the price paid for the goodwill of a practice. This was a disadvantage to a buyer who was unable to obtain a tax deduction for the value of the goodwill until they sold the asset.

Buyers and sellers will frequently have difficulty in agreeing upon how to allocate the purchase price among the assets being transferred. A seller will normally want more of the purchase price to be allocated to goodwill, rather than to tangible assets, to minimize recapture and maximize capital gains. The buyer, conversely, will want to allocate more of the purchase price to tangible assets and less to goodwill in order to accelerate his or her write-offs.

Another issue that is applicable in many states is the transfer tax arising on the sale of assets. Most states or localities assess transfer taxes against the non-inventory hard assets. The types of taxes and the rates vary from state to state and locality to locality. It is important that a seller specify in the asset purchase agreement that these transfer taxes be paid by the buyer. The responsible party for these taxes is negotiable, but as general rule, the buyer should be required to pay.

ASSET SALE STRUCTURES

Pros: • Permit buyer to pick and choose assets to purchase
       • Permit buyer to pick and choose liabilities

Cons: • Require that seller pay tax on recapture of depreciation
       • Are subject to transfer taxes

Stock Sale Structures

The principal difference between an asset sale and a stock sale is that in a sale of stock, a buyer buys an interest in the entire business of the selling veterinary practice. This is in contrast to an asset sale, where a buyer is picking and choosing the assets he or she wants to buy. Stock sale structures are utilized in many different situations when the seller is a corporation. Such structures are used when a buyer is buying the entire ownership interest of a selling veterinarian. These structures are also utilized when one of the remaining veterinarians is buying out the interest of a retiring or separating veterinarian. Stock sales are also used when an associate is buying into a practice by stair-step purchases of a selling veterinarian's ownership interest in a practice. These structures can also be utilized when a veterinary practice is expanding and adding an additional owner.

A risk with buying stock in a corporate practice is that an unknown claim or contingent liability could appear after you purchased your stock, thereby reducing the value of the stock. The stock sale transaction documents will require that a seller disclose to the buyer any debts and other liabilities. Unfortunately, this is not always an effective remedy for a buyer because the buyer could be forced to sue the seller if the seller does not agree to compensate the buyer for the liability. In addition, if the seller was not aware of the liability, the buyer has no claim against the seller. This is in contrast to an asset sale where a buyer will take steps to obligate himself only to buy specific identified assets and specific liabilities. The buyer will specify in the contract that he or she will not assume other liabilities of the selling veterinary practice and will require a selling veterinarian to comply with the necessary procedures to insulate the buyer from these liabilities.

A buyer will generally utilize one of three structures for the purchase of stock in a veterinary practice. The first and second approaches are normally, though not always, used when a buyer is buying 100 percent of the stock of a practice.

The first option is when a buyer makes a direct purchase of the stock from one or more shareholders of the practice. This option requires the buyer to enter into an individual transaction between the buyer and the selling stockholder or stockholders. It is commonly referred to as a "voluntary stock sale" because all parties have agreed to the transaction.

The second approach, which is available in most states, is when the buyer acquires the stock of the corporation in a statutory stock exchange. This procedure requires a vote of the directors and shareholders of the selling corporation and provides a certain degree of protection for the shareholders of the selling corporation. In this type of structure, all of the selling corporation's stockholders are forced to sell if the requisite votes by the directors and shareholders approve the plan. There are certain limitations to this structure. Specifically, individual stockholders of the selling practice have certain statutory rights if the corporation's directors and shareholders approve this structure.

The third approach is when a buyer acquires newly issued stock in the corporation. This frequently requires that the stockholders and board of directors of the corporation approve the issuance of the new stock and decide what percentage of the practice they want the new owner to acquire. The stockholders and board of directors must then authorize the issuance of the stock to the buyer. This structure is frequently utilized when the practice is expanding and needs to add an additional veterinarian.

Existing stockholders of a practice are adversely affected by a practice issuing new stock to a veterinarian who is buying into the practice. A veterinarian who does not want to sell his or her stock in the practice will still see a reduction in the percentage of his or her ownership interest if the corporation issues more stock. This reduction in percentage of ownership of the practice is called "dilution." A veterinarian can find him- or herself in this position if he or she does not own a majority of the stock in a practice. All states provide for a provision in the corporation's formation document that prevents dilution. However, this provision is not commonly used because it reduces the majority stockholder's ability to conduct succession planning.

There are also benefits to existing stockholders when an associate is brought into a practice through the issuance of new stock. If a veterinary practice wants to finance expansion of its facility, it can achieve this, at least partially, through the issuance of stock to a new veterinarian. By financing an expansion through the issuance of new stock, the existing veterinarians will receive the benefit of the expansion without having to assume additional debt. The downside, of course, is that the existing veterinarians will own less of the practice, but if the expansion is successful, the value of the practice should increase.

The existing stockholders will also benefit from having an additional owner to fund a buy-out if one of the veterinarians dies, becomes disabled, or retires. The expansion of the practice with an additional owner through the issuance of stock to a new veterinarian establishes a succession plan for the remaining stockholders.

That a buyer would want to purchase all of the outstanding issued stock of a practice is not unusual. A problem can develop, however, when a minority stockholder refuses to agree to sell his or her stock. This issue will be controlled by the terms of the stockholder agreement among the owners. However, if no stockholders agreement exists, the buyer has two options. First, he or she can insist that the majority stockholders attempt to conduct a statutory stock exchange. If this cannot be structured, the buyer can decide to tolerate the minority stockholder or attempt to squeeze the minority stockholder out. With few exceptions, a majority stockholder (one who owns more than 50 percent of the issued stock) controls the selection of the board of directors and the actions of the corporation. The effect of this is that the minority stockholder will not have any legal right to control the actions or direction of the veterinary practice. This is not a desirable position for the minority shareholder and will normally influence the minority stockholder to sell his or her shares.

Any transaction involving a security, such as stock in a corporate veterinary practice, must comply with state and federal securities laws. This requires that the stock be registered stock or fall within an exception or exemption under state and federal laws. A veterinarian must seek legal advice for compliance with securities laws before entering into any stock sale transaction.

Sellers of stock in a veterinary practice operating either as a "C" or an "S" corporation receive favorable tax treatment. The tax effect to a selling veterinarian of stock in a "C" corporation will be that any gain is taxed at capital gain rates. This rate, especially if held long enough to be classified as long-term capital gains, will normally be substantially less then the veterinarian's individual income tax rate.

The tax effect will change if the selling veterinarian's practice is operated as an "S" corporation. Sellers of stock in a practice operating as an "S" corporation will be required to pay tax on the recapture of depreciation taken by the corporation. This is the same tax treatment that sellers of assets receive. It is important that a tax allocation agreement be entered into between a buyer and seller to avoid the Internal Revenue Service attempting to force the seller to recapture all of the depreciation that the corporation deducted as opposed to the value of the depreciated assets. The tax allocation agreement would be used by a seller to justify the amount of the recapture tax that must be paid. The seller's gain that exceeds the recapture on the depreciation will be taxed as capital gains.

The buying veterinarian needs to be aware of the tax effect of a stock purchase. A buying veterinarian of stock is not entitled to depreciate the purchase price for the stock as he or she would have if he or she had purchased assets. The buyer can, however, retain a high tax basis in the stock and, depending upon the transaction, could be able to retain the net operating loss (NOL) carry forward with the corporation. However, the transfer of more than 50 percent of the corporate stock eliminates the opportunity to utilize the loss carry forward. A benefit for a buying veterinarian with a stock sale is that this could avoid a use or transfer tax upon the sale that may be present in an asset sale.

The options for structuring a stock sale succession plan will also vary depending upon whether the buyer is buying a partial interest in an existing practice or buying all of the outstanding stock of a veterinary practice. The structure for the sale of all of the stock interest in a practice will normally be much more straightforward than will the structure of an associate buying into a practice.

A stock sale structure where the seller is leaving the practice eliminates the need to establish the legal working relationship between the buyer and the selling stockholders. There may, of course, be more than one owner of the buying business organization, which would require the structuring of the owners' relationship. This issue, however, is not a concern for a seller and is not addressed in the succession plan transaction documents.

A stock sale structure where an existing veterinarian wishes to exit his or her practice at some point in the future can be very simple or very complicated. Frequently, this type of structure involves a selling veterinarian who wants to sell a portion of his or her interest in the practice in order to establish his or her succession plan. The selling veterinarian will want to contractually bind the buyer to purchase the seller's remaining interest when he or she is ready to retire.

This type of structure requires detailed analysis of the goals of the buyer and the seller in order to structure a legal relationship that will meet the objectives of both veterinarians.

This stock sale becomes more complicated when a buyer does not have the financial ability to purchase the seller's stock without the seller financing the purchase price. Depending upon the value of the practice, this may create difficulties in structuring a purchase so that the seller will have had most of his or her interest purchased and paid off before exiting the practice. This is especially a problem when the value of the practice is so high that the buyer cannot generate enough cash from his or her production and ownership in the practice to pay the monthly payments for the purchase of the stock and his or her living expenses. In this situation, a seller either needs to accept the fact that it will take a long-term payment structure to complete a succession plan with this buyer or that he or she will have no choice but to find another buyer.

If a seller of stock agrees to finance the purchase over a long term, the transaction will normally be structured to permit the buyer to buy the seller's stock in small increments. The succession plan will require that the buyer pay the purchase price for each stock increment in full before buying the next increment of stock. Unlike a structure that is designed to permit a seller to be bought out when he or she is ready to retire, this plan will normally establish deadlines for when the buyer will be required to have purchased all of the seller's stock. Although this would appear to limit a seller, it actually benefits the seller by establishing deadlines for the buyer to have paid the seller for his or her stock. In addition, in this type of structure, the seller is normally forced to accept payments over eight to ten years, and that is normally longer than the seller wants to practice.

This stock sale should also be structured to obligate the buyer to purchase the entire remaining stock interest when the next increment would give the buyer a majority stock interest. This protects the seller in that it prevents the buyer from having control over the practice without having bought out the entire stock interest of the seller. The sale can also be structured, if the seller so desires, to require the corporation to hire the seller as an associate for a certain number of years after he or she sells the final increment of stock. The term of this employment agreement can parallel the term of the promissory note on the final stock purchase, or it can be structured to permit the seller to keep working until he or she is ready to retire.

STOCK SALE STRUCTURES

Pros: • Offer flexible options
           • Receive favorable tax treatment

Cons:- • Require buyers of stock to take it subject to liabilities of practice
           • Involve complicated tax issues that require planning

---

Installment Payment Structures

Almost all transactions involving the sale of a veterinary practice require a selling veterinarian to accept a promissory note as partial, if not full, payment for the purchase of the practice. The promissory note will normally charge the buyer an annual interest rate for the outstanding balance of the note and obligate the buyer to make monthly payments until the principal and interest are paid in full.

The reason that the majority of sellers of veterinary practices are forced to finance the purchase is because of the difficulty in obtaining loans for the purchase. It would be much easier to structure veterinary succession plan transactions if traditional lenders, i.e., banks, finance companies, were willing to lend money for purchases of assets or stock of a veterinary practice. Unfortunately, traditional lenders are hesitant to lend money for the purchase of veterinary practices without substantial collateral to secure the obligation above and beyond the assets or stock being purchased. Many of the structures that are discussed in this book have been utilized because a buyer could not pay a substantial amount of cash up front.

Sellers that are unable to locate qualified buyers to implement a succession plan will frequently be faced with either financing the sale or not having a buyer. The practical effect of this is that the seller will also have very little control over the length of time that the buyer has to pay the obligation. The length of time that a buyer will have to pay his or her promissory note obligations is frequently influenced more by the cash flow of the practice than the desires of the seller. A payment plan is frequently determined by estimating the cash flow of the practice and reducing that amount by the operational expenses of the practice and owner compensation. That amount is then reduced by an amount that will permit the buyer to maintain an acceptable standard of living during the payment plan term. The remaining estimated revenue is the disposable revenue available to pay the seller for the purchase.

Sellers are frequently frustrated that they do not have more control over the transaction. Their frustration is understandable; however, if a seller cannot find a buyer who can pay a large down payment, the seller will be forced to accept the amount that can feasibly be paid by a buyer. It does not benefit a seller to have a buyer enter into an agreement that he or she cannot honor. It will only place the seller in a more difficult position at a later date.

Most buying veterinarians make the payments required by the promissory notes without defaulting. However, there are times when a buyer does not make the payments as he or she had agreed. When this happens, a selling veterinarian learns how well his or her lawyer structured the succession plan transaction documents. It is unfortunate, but a seller will not know if the attorney protected his or her interests in a transaction until the documents are challenged in a court of law.

If the transaction was properly negotiated to place the selling veterinarian as a priority or first-in-line secured creditor, and the transaction documents and post-transaction filings were properly completed, then the selling veterinarian should have the legal right to seize the practice. If, however, the transaction documents did not protect the selling veterinarian's interest, then the selling veterinarian may find him- or herself without the right to seize the practice in the event of a default. If this happens, the seller will be limited to filing a lawsuit to recover monetary damages without the immediate right to seize assets of the practice.

It is also important to understand that you are not guaranteed a good result even if you do have the legal right to seize the assets of the practice. Some veterinarians want their buyer to default so that they can keep the money that they have been paid and then resell the practice to another veterinarian. At first this might appear to be a profitable option. There are, however, several reasons why seizing the practice may not solve a seller's problems.

The laws of many states do not permit a seller to seize the assets of a practice after a default and take the practice over again. The laws of these states will either prevent a seller from keeping the seized assets or prevent the seller who kept the seized assets from suing to recover on the unpaid balance of the promissory note. A seller must analyze whether there is any benefit to retaining the right to sue on the unpaid balance of the promissory note. If there is little chance of recovering from the buyer after the buyer loses the practice, it may make sense to enter into an agreement in which the seller takes back the assets and releases the buyer from his or her obligations under the promissory note.

Another reason why seizing the practice when a buyer fails to make payments may not be the best option is if the production of the practice has substantially fallen since the buyer took control. If the practice has seen a substantial reduction in gross revenues, it is unlikely that the seller could immediately resell the practice for an amount close to the original sales price. A seller would need to either come back to the practice to build it up again or find a qualified associate to build up the practice for him or her.

There are of course times when the seller will have no choice but to seize the practice or negotiate with the buyer and have him or her turn the practice back over to the seller. However, if a seller does not want to spend the time and money to build the practice back up, it may be better for the seller to analyze why the buyer is failing before making a decision. If the seller determines that it is a problem that the buyer can overcome, it might be a better decision for the seller to restructure the debt or get involved with the operations of the practice to help the buyer succeed.

INSTALLMENT PAYMENT STRUCTURES

Pros: • Create flexibility to assist seller in locating a buyer to complete succession plan

Cons: • Require seller to delay receiving payment for purchase price
• Presents seller with risk of not being paid by buyer and having to take practice back from buyer

Pre-Tax Salary Reduction Payment Structure

Buyers of veterinary practices frequently want the purchase price to be paid for through a pre-tax salary reduction plan. This type of plan is sometimes utilized when a seller remains with the practice after a stock sale. The plan is structured so that the stock purchase agreement shows a small purchase price, with the seller receiving the true value through a shifting of the buyer's wages to the seller. The buyer and seller will normally enter into employment agreements with the veterinary practice that reflect what their base wages are after shifting the income to the seller. The employment agreement will specify the term of the agreement, which will correspond with the payment of the remaining purchase price. The wages of the buyer and seller will be modified after the seller has been fully compensated for the true value of the stock.

This type of a structure is considered a buyer-friendly provision because the buyer will pay for the stock with pre-tax dollars. It is a pretax dollar structure because the buyer has not had to receive his or her wages from the corporation with the reduction for payroll taxes and individual income taxes. This will permit the buyer to pay off the seller much more quickly than would normally occur.

A seller will not receive favorable tax treatment with this structure because he or she will be paying individual income taxes and payroll taxes on the money. If the seller was selling "C" corporation stock and he or she had forced the buyer to pay for the stock with money that the buyer received as wages, the seller would have received capital gains tax treatment. This would have provided the seller with a significant increase in after-tax gains from the sale of stock. If the seller was selling "S" corporation stock, he or she would have first been liable for the recapture on the depreciation from the hard assets but would have been able to take the remaining gain as a capital gain.

There are significant problems with this structure. One of the most significant is that the Internal Revenue Service does not approve of such a transaction. If it can establish that the buyer was entitled to more wages and chose to not take the wages, it will restructure the transaction and impose taxes and penalties. This could also cause significant problems if the practice has a pension plan based on the amount of wage compensation.

PRE-TAX SALARY REDUCTION STRUCTURE

Pros: • Buyer is permitted to pay for purchase price with pre-tax dollars
       • Flexibility is created to assist seller in locating a buyer to complete succession plan

Cons: • Internal Revenue Service may challenge transaction
       • Purchase price for stock is not realistic of value of stock
       • Seller loses tax benefits of stock sale
       • Seller could lose income if it is being shifted as income and seller is unable to continue to practice

---

Liquidation and Sale of Assets

A variation on a traditional asset sale from a corporation is to have a corporation liquidate first and distribute all of its assets to its shareholders. A liquidation will require that the shareholders either pay or otherwise make provisions for the payment of liabilities of the corporation. Upon the liabilities of the corporation being taken care of, the corporation can be legally liquidated and have the assets distributed to the shareholders. The shareholders, or some of the shareholders, can then in their individual capacity decide which assets they choose to sell. This type of structure can accomplish a succession plan if some of the owners of the selling practice have different goals and want to retain certain assets to start up their own practice. It is not, however, a common structure because a buyer will not want to buy assets of a practice unless all of the veterinarians in the practice agree to enter into an agreement in which they will not solicit the clients or compete with the buyer. If there is an individual veterinarian who does not want to sell the assets, that veterinarian will normally want to compete with the new owner. This will effectively prevent this structure from being used.

LIQUIDATION AND SALE OF ASSETS

Pros: • Allows partial asset sale when owners or seller cannot agree to authorize asset sale

Cons: • Requires all stockholders of seller to agree to not compete with buyer

Selecting the Appropriate Legal Structure for Succession Planning

4

Veterinarians are frequently concerned with whether they are utilizing the "best" legal structure or business organization. All too often, however, discussions veterinarians have about the "best" business organization for their practice are limited to what will provide the best immediate tax benefit or the best shield from liability. Veterinarians frequently fail to consider whether the legal structure that they are choosing is the "best" business organization for succession planning purposes.

A proper analysis of the business organization for a veterinary practice involves a three-step analysis.

The first step that must be undertaken is an evaluation of the tax effects of the various legal structures and how each structure will affect the veterinarian's individual finances. It is imperative that this analysis be tailored to the individual owner's finances. If this is not done, the veterinarian may be in for an unpleasant surprise that could easily have been avoided.

The second step requires an analysis of the applicable state laws regarding the various business organizations. A veterinarian must understand whether or not their selection of business organization places their individual assets at risk. A veterinarian must also determine whether their state's veterinary practice act permits the practice of veterinary medicine through their selection of a business organization.

The third step is to analyze the business organization's options for succession planning purposes. It is important that a veterinarian analyze the advantages and disadvantages of each legal structure from a succession planning standpoint. Some of the issues that must be considered when analyzing a business organization for succession planning purposes are: whether the business organization can be structured with multiple owners and what the options are for such a structure under each state's laws; what the current tax effect is for the transfer of an ownership interest under the various types of business organizations; and how the various business organizations can be structured to permit their continuation if an owner dies or becomes disabled.

Historically, veterinarians have been limited in their business organization options. The only standard options available to veterinarians were sole proprietorship, general partnership, limited partnership, and corporation. In most states the 1990s have been a period of time when veterinarians' business organization options have greatly expanded. Most veterinary medical practice acts now permit veterinarians to operate as a limited liability company and limited liability partnership. A few states have also permitted veterinarians to adopt forms of business that are a variation on these forms.

It is important for veterinarians to understand that with the proliferation of business organization options, there will be many cases when there is more than one option that could be the "right" business organization for a specific veterinarian. The difference between some of the options may be very minimal depending upon the veterinarian's specific financial situation.

The issues facing a veterinarian who is selecting a business organization or considering restructuring are complicated and involved. Errors can easily be made that the veterinarian will not even be aware of until he or she is attempting to sell his or her practice. These errors can sometimes cost thousands and thousands of dollars. An example of this is a veterinary practice operating as a "C" corporation that bought and developed real estate to operate the practice. Over a number of years the real estate dramatically increased in value. When the stockholders began their succession planning, they discovered that their corporation would have a very large tax liability upon the sale of the real estate. They learned that this tax liability would have been substantially reduced if they had either owned the real estate individually and leased it to the practice or been an "S" corporation. It is important that veterinarians seek competent advisers to help them through this process.

SELECTING THE APPROPRIATE LEGAL STRUCTURES

Pros: • Expands understanding of business organization options
• Creates options to maximize tax and legal benefits of business organization for personal finances of veterinarian

Cons: • Can be complicated by too much information - sensory overload
• Can be difficult because no one business organization is a "best" legal organization
• Requires more support by experts

Sole Proprietorship or Sole Ownership

What is a sole proprietorship?

A sole proprietorship is nothing more than a one-owner practice. If a practice acquires a second owner, it automatically ceases to be a sole proprietorship and becomes a partnership.

What are the legal formalities to operate as a sole proprietorship?

There are no legal formalities to be recognized as a sole proprietorship. Under most state laws, all that is required of a veterinarian to practice as a sole proprietor is to open the door and begin operating a practice. This is in stark contrast to corporations and limited liability companies that are not recognized as a legal entity until the appropriate documents have been filed in compliance with the state laws.

Who manages a sole proprietorship?

The owner of a sole proprietorship has complete control over the management of the business. As previously stated, in order for a veterinary practice to be recognized as a sole proprietorship, there can be only one owner.

Who is responsible for debts of a veterinary practice operating as a sole proprietorship?

The owner of a veterinary practice operating as a sole proprietorship is individually responsible for any and all liabilities of the practice. The owner does not have a shield or any protection from individual liability as a sole proprietor. The effect of this is that a creditor of a sole proprietorship is entitled to file suit against the individual owner, and if successful in obtaining a judgment, to seize individual assets of the owner to satisfy or pay the obligations of the practice.

A veterinarian who is operating a practice as a sole proprietorship can minimize the risk of his or her personal assets being seized by obtaining professional liability and general liability insurance. Many of the risks that arise from the operation of a veterinary practice can be insured, thereby protecting the owner's individual assets from seizure by a creditor. Unfortunately, no insurance policy will protect one from all potential liabilities that can occur with a veterinary practice. There is no insurance that will insure and defend a veterinarian from a lawsuit by a landlord for failure to pay his or her commercial office space rent. It is important that a veterinarian analyze his or her practice to determine whether he or she should operate the practice as a sole proprietorship or select a business organization that will provide a shield from individual liability.

How is a sole proprietorship taxed?

Veterinarians who operate as sole proprietors must report the profits or losses of their veterinary practice to the Internal Revenue Service. The profits from the operation of the practice will be taxed at the individual income tax rate of the owner. Generally, sole proprietors are entitled to take tax deductions and depreciation on their assets like other business organizations.

Veterinarians who operate as sole proprietorships do not file a separate tax return for their practice. The Internal Revenue Service requires sole proprietorships to file an Internal Revenue Form Schedule "C" as an attachment or schedule to the individual owner's Form 1040 tax return. This is in contrast to corporations, partnerships, and limited liability companies, which are required to file a separate tax return. The benefit of not having to file a separate tax return will save the owner a substantial sum of money for the cost of tax return preparation over the life of the practice.

A significant tax issue for sole proprietors is that all profits of their practices are subject to self-employment tax in addition to their individual state and federal income tax rates. Self-employment taxes are similar in amount to the taxes that businesses withhold and match for employee salaries.

Is a sole proprietorship a good succession planning vehicle?

Operating a veterinary practice as a sole proprietorship has some definite advantages. As a succession planning vehicle, however, a sole proprietorship has some disadvantages. A sole proprietorship limits a seller's options for succession planning. A sole proprietorship can legally have only one owner. If the veterinary practice adds another owner, it automatically becomes a partnership. This prevents a selling veterinarian from bringing in an additional owner as part of a succession plan without restructuring his or her practice under a different business organization.

A selling veterinarian will not care if his or her options are limited if he or she is able to find a buyer of his or her assets. The problem that many veterinarians encounter is that a buyer of their assets may not appear when they are ready to sell. If this happens, the selling veterinarian may be forced to restructure his or her practice into another business organization in order to structure an associate buy-in of some form.

A sole proprietorship is also an unpopular option for succession planning because the owner of the practice does not have a shield from practice liabilities. A creditor can sue the owner and take the owner's individual assets to satisfy the practice's obligations.

Another reason why a sole proprietorship is not a good succession planning vehicle is because it does not provide for the continuity of the business upon the death or disability of the owner. When a sole proprietor dies or becomes disabled, he or she does not have a structure providing for the purchase of his or her interest by a co-owner. This problem is exasperated when a state's veterinary practice act does not permit non-veterinarians to own veterinary practices. A relative of a deceased veterinarian who inherits the practice is likely to lose a large percentage of the value of the practice upon the death of the sole proprietor owner because the practice will have to be sold on an emergency "fire sale" basis. This situation could be avoided if there were multiple owners with agreements structured to maximize the value for the inheriting relatives.

SOLE PROPRIETORSHIP OR SOLE OWNERSHIP

Pros: • Is simple to form and maintain
- Provides complete control over decisions affecting the practice

Cons: • Holds owner personally liable for obligations of practice
- Is a self-employment tax liability
- Offers no assurance of the continuity of the business after the death or disability of the owner

---

Partnerships/Limited Partnerships

What is a partnership?

Veterinarians who operate a practice with more than one owner are considered general partners in a general partnership. Under most state laws, a general partnership exists when two or more individuals operate a business for profit. A sole proprietorship that adds an owner immediately loses its status as a sole proprietorship and becomes a general partnership as a matter of law.

What is a limited partnership?

A limited partnership is a partnership with at least one general partner and with one or more limited partners. All state limited partnership laws require that there be at least one general partner in a limited partnership who is personally liable for the debts of the partnership.

What are the legal formalities to operate a veterinary practice as a general partnership?

Most states' laws do not impose any formal requirements to be recognized as a general partnership. These laws do not even require that there be a written partnership agreement. There are, however, pitfalls for veterinarians who do not understand the legal effect of operating a general partnership without a formal partnership agreement. Under most states' laws, general partners in a general partnership who have not entered into a formal partnership agreement share the profits and losses of the practice equally. This poses a problem when an owner of a practice brings a younger veterinarian into the practice with the verbal understanding that the older, more established veterinarian will receive a larger share of the profits. This verbal agreement, if denied by the younger veterinarian, could be very difficult to enforce. This is especially true if a problem develops between the two veterinarians and the younger veterinarian files a lawsuit to force the older veterinarian to pay the younger one his or her one-half of the profits for the period of time that the younger veterinarian was practicing with the older one. The older veterinarian is only protected if he or she has a written agreement clarifying the distribution of profits and losses among the partners.

What are the formalities required to operate a veterinary practice as a limited partnership?

Most states' laws require certain formalities to operate as a limited partnership. However, these formalities are generally very limited and do not compare with the formalities of operating as a corporation or limited liability company. Although most state laws do not require that a written limited partnership agreement exist, it is advisable to have one. A limited partnership is designed to limit the liability of the individual limited partners. The limited partners are at risk to be sued by creditors claiming that the partners are general partners liable for the debts of the practice. This can only be avoided if the partners have a well-drafted agreement clarifying their role as limited partners.

Who manages a general partnership?

Generally, a partnership is operated and managed by its partners. However, the owners or partners of a general partnership can designate a manager to handle the affairs of the entity.

Who manages a limited partnership?

Limited partnerships are generally managed by one or more general partners. Limited partners are generally required to have minimal involvement in the management of the limited partnership in order to retain their shield from individual liability.

Who is responsible for liabilities of a veterinary practice operating as a general partnership?

General partners are individually liable for all obligations of the general partnership when the assets of the general partnership are not adequate to pay the obligation. There is no shield from liability as a general partner. This individual liability is termed "joint and several liability" and permits a creditor to collect the entire debt from one partner regardless of his or her actual percentage of ownership in the company. The general partner who is forced to pay the entire obligation would then have the legal right to seek recovery from the remaining partners for their respective share of the obligation.

Who is responsible for liabilities of a veterinary practice operating as a limited partnership?

All general partners of limited partnerships are personally responsible for debts of a limited partnership. Limited partners generally are not individually liable for the limited partnership's liabilities and will only lose their investment in the practice.

This insulation of liability for limited partners is frequently prohibited by veterinary practice acts for malpractice claims against the individual veterinarian. However, the veterinary practice acts do not prohibit a veterinarian from limiting his or her personal liability from non-malpractice claims. Further, a veterinarian operating as a limited partner in a limited partnership can shield his or her individual assets by obtaining malpractice insurance with adequate policy limits.

How is a general partnership taxed?

Partnerships are pass-through business entities that file a tax return but pass the gains and losses to the owners or partners who pay the tax. The effect of this is that the partnership will not pay income tax on its profits. Each owner in the partnership receives a tax statement from the partnership called a K-1 that declares the individual tax liability for his or her share of the profits or losses of the partnership.

How is a limited partnership taxed?

Limited partnerships must qualify under the Internal Revenue Code to be taxed as a pass-through business entity to pass the gains and losses on to the owners. If the partnership agreement is not properly drafted, the limited partnership could be taxed as an association (which is taxed in the same manner as a corporation).

Are general partnerships and limited partnerships good succession planning vehicles?

A properly structured general partnership can be a flexible succession planning vehicle. The general partnership is also a good succession planning business organization because it can be structured to establish procedures to be followed if the retirement, death, disability, or bankruptcy of a partner occurs. A well-drafted general partnership agreement will generally permit flexibility in adding additional owners to a practice to permit the structuring of an associate buy-in of some form.

Although a general partnership can be a flexible succession planning business organization, the fact that all general partners are individually liable for the obligations of the general partnership makes it undesirable. The creation of limited liability companies with their insulation from owner liability has made the use of general partnerships in succession planning a rare event.

Limited partnerships have limited application in succession planning for veterinary practices. Under most state laws, limited partners must limit their involvement in the management of the company to retain their limited shield from liability. This creates a problem because a buyer in a succession plan will want to be involved in the management of the practice. The creation of limited liability companies has eliminated the use for limited partnerships in veterinary practice succession planning.

PARTNERSHIPS & LIMITED PARTNERSHIPS

Pros: • Are easier and less complicated to create and form than corporations or limited liability companies
       • Can receive flow-through federal tax treatment, which is generally a favorable tax treatment

Cons: • Holds general partners liable for all debts of the partnership
       • Can be formed without the individuals intending to be a partnership

---

Corporations

What is a corporation?

A corporation is a business organization that is recognized as a legal entity upon compliance with the state's formal requirements.

What are the formalities required to operate as a corporation?

All states require that certain formalities be followed to be recognized as a corporation. Most states require that applicants file articles of incorporation or certificates of incorporation to be considered to operate as a corporation. The information contained within these documents will vary from state to state. All states require that the corporation adopts bylaws for the day-to-day governance of the entity and that it complies with certain periodic formalities in order to continue to be recognized as a corporation.

If an applicant begins operating a practice without having been recognized as a corporation, the operation will be treated as either a sole proprietorship or a partnership, depending upon the number of owners.

Who manages a corporation?

A corporation is controlled by shareholders who elect a board of directors. The board of directors will either manage the day-to-day affairs of the practice or hire a manager to operate the practice. The ultimate decision-making authority lies with the board of directors.

Who is liable for the debts of the corporation?

A stockholder of a corporation is generally insulated from the liabilities of the corporation. However, there are certain exceptions to this. Veterinary practice acts frequently prohibit veterinarians from insulation for malpractice claims. The effect of this can be minimized by a veterinarian operating his or her practice as a corporation by obtaining malpractice insurance with adequate policy limits.

Another exception to the general rule occurs when a stockholder personally guarantees a corporate liability. If the practice is unable to pay an obligation that the veterinarian individually guaranteed, the veterinarian will be liable for the debt.

There are additional circumstances when courts will permit creditors to pierce the corporate veil and hold stockholders individually liable for debts of their corporations. The elements that must be proven to permit a creditor from doing this vary from state to state. However, the following elements could justify a creditor attempting to pierce the corporate veil:

✓ lack of a separate identity
✓ inadequate capitalization
✓ illegal purpose
✓ fraud
✓ other equitable factors
✓ failure to comply with corporate formalities

It is also notable that the Internal Revenue Service can pierce the corporate veil and seize individual assets of the shareholders for unpaid payroll withholding taxes.

How is a corporation taxed?

All corporations must file separate tax returns. However, corporations are taxed differently depending upon whether or not the shareholders have elected and qualified to be taxed as a "C" or an "S" corporation. The selection of "S" or "C" tax treatment by a corporation's shareholders is simply a tax election and does not affect the shareholders' shield from individual liability.

What is an "S" corporation and how is it taxed?

"S" corporations are flow-through entities for federal income tax purposes. Flow-through tax treatment means that the corporation is obligated to declare to the Internal Revenue Service the amount of taxable income that each shareholder is liable to pay taxes on based upon his or her ownership interest and the total amount of taxable income for the corporation. This income is taxable regardless of whether the corporation disbursed the profits to permit the shareholders to pay their taxes.

One of the benefits of "S" corporations for veterinarians is that, in most cases, the Internal Revenue Service permits a veterinarian to disburse a portion of his or her income from the corporation as an "S" corporation profit. The effect of classifying a portion of the income as an "S" corporation profit is that the income will be taxed to the veterinarian as ordinary income subject only to state and federal income tax and not subject to payroll taxes or self-employment tax. This is a substantial benefit that the Internal Revenue Service does not permit most other business organizations to do. The Internal Revenue Service will not permit you to take all of your income out of the "S" corporation as an "S" corporation profit. Instead, the IRS requires veterinarians to disburse a portion of their income from their "S" corporation as W-2 wages with payroll tax withholdings. The Internal Revenue Service also requires that the amount of the W-2 wage to be disbursed to the veterinarian be based upon an amount that a veterinarian would be paid if he or she were an employee. This is an issue that is subject to dispute if your practice was to be audited by the IRS.

An "S" corporation is limited in the number and type of stockholders. An "S" corporation is generally limited in that it

✓ may not have more than 35 shareholders
✓ may not have corporations, partnerships, or some trusts as shareholders
✓ may not have a nonresident alien as a shareholder
✓ may not have more than one class of stock
✓ may not be a regulated investment company or real estate investment trust, nor be part of an affiliated group

What is a "C" corporation and how is it taxed?

A "C" corporation is a business organization that retains its own profits and losses and is taxed as a separate entity from its shareholders. The "C" corporation is required to pay federal and state taxes on its profits. Veterinary practices operating as "C" corporations are classified as personal service corporations by the Internal Revenue Code. The effect of this classification is that the corporation will pay an income tax rate of 34 percent.

A common problem for stockholders in "C" corporations is "double-taxation." If a "C" corporation shows a profit at the end of its fiscal or calendar year, it will be required to pay corporate income taxes on the gain. If the corporation subsequently disburses the previous year's profits that it paid corporate taxes upon to its shareholders as wages, the gain is subject to federal and state income taxes as well as payroll taxes. The income that has been disbursed to the stockholders has been subjected to both corporate and individual taxes.

Is a corporation a good succession plan vehicle?

Corporations are very good succession plan vehicles because they are flexible entities. Corporations provide for a shield from individual liability for the owners of the practice. This is an option that will be attractive to either an associate buying in or a third party purchasing the stock of an existing owner.

Corporations are also attractive succession plan vehicles because they can establish procedures to be followed if the retirement, death, disability, or bankruptcy of a partner occurs. This type of structure will protect the interests of a selling veterinarian in the event that he or she is unable to continue to practice after having an associate begin buying into the practice.

Corporations also provide a great deal of tax planning flexibility, depending upon the type of structure being utilized.

It is frequently a benefit for a seller of a veterinary practice under a succession plan to sell stock in a "C" corporation. If the seller of the stock has owned the stock long enough to qualify under the long-term capital gains rules, the seller will be taxed by the federal government on the gain from the sale of his or her stock at a tax rate that is frequently a reduction from the veterinarian's individual income tax rate. This is why succession plans are frequently structured as stock sales as opposed to asset sales.

The tax treatment will be different if the corporation has elected to be treated as an "S" corporation. Under the laws of the Internal Revenue Service as of publication of this book, a sale of stock in an "S" corporation will be taxed differently than the sale of stock in a "C" corporation. An owner of stock in an "S" corporation will generally not receive capital gains treatment on the entire gain from the sale of his or her stock. A seller of "S" corporation stock will be forced to pay tax on recaptured depreciation that the "S" corporation deducted from the purchase of assets that are currently owned by the "S" corporation. The gain above and beyond the taxable recaptured depreciation will be taxed as a capital gain.

In order to maximize the capital gain tax treatment and minimize the recapture of depreciation, it is important that the stock purchase agreement entered into between the parties identifies a tax allocation for the purchase price, thereby designating the taxable value of the asset that is subject to taxable recapture of depreciation. This will prevent the Internal Revenue Service from taking a position in the audit that the value of the depreciated assets was higher then their fair market value. This, in turn, has the effect of minimizing the taxable recapture of depreciation.

CORPORATIONS

Pros: • Provide insulation from stockholder liability
• Have flexible options for taxation
• Are flexible succession planning vehicles

Cons: • Are complicated to form and maintain
• Require understanding of tax laws to avoid bad results

Limited Liability Companies

What is a limited liability company?

All states and the District of Columbia have adopted laws to permit the formation of a business entity known as a limited liability company. These business entities are designed to accomplish two specific goals. The first goal is to provide owners and members of the limited liability company with limited personal liability. The second goal is to confer upon the owners the preferential income tax treatment of a pass-through entity.

Prior to the adoption of state laws permitting the formation of limited liability companies, veterinarians had the option of forming a corporation to obtain the shield from individual liability. A veterinarian could also form a general partnership in order to obtain the pass-through tax treatment. However, there was no one single entity that offered both of these advantages.

What are the formalities required to create a limited liability company?

A limited liability company is a business organization that requires specific formalities be followed to receive state recognition. The formalities are similar to the formalities of forming a corporation. A limited liability company can only be formed by the filing of the proper documents, usually called Articles of Organization, with the proper governmental organization.

Who is responsible for liabilities of a limited liability company?

Owners of limited liability companies (referred to as members) are individually insulated from the liabilities of the practice. This means that if the limited liability is unable to pay its creditors, creditors are not permitted to pursue the owners for payment. This is the same type of shield from liability that shareholders of corporations enjoy. In fact, the majority of the limited liability statutes expressly adopted the shield from liability court rulings from their state to apply to limited liability companies.

There are certain exceptions to this general insulation from liability. Veterinary practice acts frequently prohibit veterinarians from insulation of individual liability for malpractice claims. However, these acts do not prohibit a veterinarian from limiting his or her personal liability from non-malpractice claims. Further, a veterinarian operating his or her practice as a limited liability company can shield his or her individual assets by obtaining malpractice insurance with adequate policy limits.

Another exception to the general rule occurs when a member personally guarantees a limited liability company liability. If the practice is unable to pay an obligation that the veterinarian individually guaranteed, the veterinarian will be liable for the debt.

How is a limited liability company taxed?

Limited liability companies were created to take advantage of the favorable tax treatment of a pass-through entity. Under this type of treatment, a veterinary practice operating as a limited liability company would not be taxed on any income it generates from its operations. Instead, all taxable revenues and expenses would be passed through to the owners of the entity who would then be responsible for the payment of the tax, if any, on those revenues and expenses.

Limited liability companies are a relatively new type of business entity. The first limited liability company state law was adopted in 1977. The majority of states did not pass legislation permitting the entity until after 1988 when a tax court ruling identified certain tests that it would focus on to determine whether a specific limited liability company was to be treated as a pass-through entity or a corporation. The reason so many states hesitated to adopt a limited liability company law was because a question existed as to whether the limited liability company would be classified as a partnership, thereby receiving preferential pass-through tax treatment, or classified and taxed as a corporation for federal tax treatment purposes. After this ruling, many states adopted their limited liability company statutes with the guidance of their knowledge of the specific test elements.

The Internal Revenue Service has replaced the case-by-case testing of whether a limited liability company is to be taxed as a pass-through entity or a corporation with a simplified elective procedure, commonly referred to as a "check-the-box" procedure. Effective January 1, 1997, depending on the number of owners of the limited liability company, owners are entitled to elect to be treated for federal tax purposes either as a corporation or as a pass-through entity. The regulation provides that a limited liability company that has two or more members can elect to be treated either as a corporation or a pass-through entity. The regulation further provides that if the limited liability company has only one member, the company can elect to be treated as a corporation or to disregard the separate entity and be taxed as a sole proprietorship.

The regulation also provides that if an election is not made, there are certain facts that would trigger a default effect. In general, if a limited liability company with two or more members does not make an election, it will receive pass-through tax treatment. Another general default under the regulation is that if a limited liability company with one member does not make an election, the Internal Revenue Service will disregard the limited liability company as an entity separate from the owner and treat it as a sole proprietorship.

Is a limited liability company a good succession planning vehicle?

A limited liability company is an excellent vehicle for a succession plan. To begin with, it provides for insulation from personal liability for existing and subsequent owners. This offers a greater level of comfort for a veterinarian considering buying into an existing veterinary practice.

Limited liability companies are also attractive succession plan vehicles because they can establish procedures to be followed if the retirement, death, disability, or bankruptcy of a member occurs. This type of structure will protect the interests of a selling veterinarian.

LIMITED LIABILITY COMPANY

Pros: • Requires that profits and losses be taxed to the member or owner as flow-through tax treatment
   • Limits liability for all owners or members
   • Is a good succession planning vehicle
   • Can be formed in certain states with only one owner or member

Cons: • Is a very formalized entity requiring filings with the state to form
   • May be taxed as a corporation without the intention of the members or owners
   • Could have its limited liability status pierced by a creditor

---

Limited Liability Partnerships

What is a limited liability partnership?

A limited liability partnership is a legal entity that is authorized by state statute. It is an entity that has come into existence only since limited liability companies became popular.

What are the formalities required to create a limited liability partnership?

Limited liability partnerships are very similar to limited liability companies in that they are similarly formed. State statutes require that a written document be created and filed with the appropriate state agency prior to the creation of the entity.

There is, however, a difference between a limited liability partnership and a limited liability company in the number of persons required to form the entity. A limited liability partnership generally requires two or more persons to be owners in order to exist. This is in contrast to a limited liability company that can exist with only one owner in some states.

Who manages a limited liability partnership?

Limited liability partnerships are generally treated differently when it comes to their management. These two entities can be treated in the same manner if their operating documents provide for similar management. However, generally a limited liability partnership is operated and managed by its partners equally. This is how general partnerships are operated and managed. This is in contrast to a limited liability company that has the legal right to have centralized management. Most state laws permit individuals who are not owners to operate and manage the entity. It is also notable that under many limited liability partnership statutes, management is required to be in proportion to the members' capital contributions.

Who is responsible for liabilities of a veterinary practice operated as a limited liability partnership?

In a limited liability partnership, the partners are generally personally liable for certain, but not all, debts and obligations for the entity. This is in contrast to a limited liability company, where owners are generally not responsible for debts of the entity. The extent of the personal liability for the owner of the limited liability partnership varies from state to state.

How is a limited liability partnership taxed?

The tax treatment for limited liability partnerships and limited liability companies is generally that of a pass-through tax entity for federal income tax purposes. Neither entity would be directly taxed but instead would pass through all profits, losses, and gains to its owners. This can be altered if the limited liability company does not qualify for flow-through tax treatment. It is also notable that even if the two entities are treated the same by the federal tax treatment, they may be treated differently for state tax purposes.

Is a limited liability partnership a good succession planning vehicle?

A limited liability partnership is not as flexible for succession planning as other entities such as limited liability companies and corporations. The insulation from liability is not as thorough under most state laws as is the insulation from liability of the other entities.

However, a limited liability partnership is a flexible vehicle for succession planning purposes to the extent that it can establish procedures to be followed if the retirement, death, disability, or bankruptcy of a member occurs. This type of structure will protect the interests of a selling veterinarian.

LIMITED LIABILITY PARTNERSHIPS

Pros: • Offers partial insulation from owner liability
            • Generally receives favorable pass-through tax treatment

Cons: • Is a very formalized entity requiring filings with the state to form
            • Is generally not a good succession planning vehicle

Contracts for Succession Planning Transactions

5

Chapter 4 described the basic types of succession planning legal structures and a few of the more common variations of these structures. This chapter goes to the next step and discusses how a veterinarian should approach preliminary discussions with a buyer or seller to avoid problems when trying to complete the succession planning transaction. This chapter also discusses the due diligence phase of the succession plan transaction and the contracts that are necessary to complete a succession planning transaction.

Buyers' and Sellers' Objectives in Succession Planning Transactions

It is important to keep in mind the respective objectives of buyers and sellers in negotiating a veterinary succession plan transaction. There are certain inherent differences in the focus and goals of a buyer versus a seller.

A buyer's primary non-tax objectives are to acquire the practice at a good price with contract terms that are favorable to the buyer. A buyer will want to feel comfortable that he or she is obtaining clear title to the practice assets or stock without being obligated for liabilities of the selling practice. In addition, a buyer will want to know that the contracts are drafted to provide him or her remedies should it later be determined that a seller misrepresented or lied about the practice. A buyer will also want to have contracts in place to prevent the seller from competing with the buyer's practice and from soliciting the client base after the sale.

A seller's primary non-tax objective is to obtain the maximum possible purchase price. The seller will want most, if not all, of the purchase price paid at closing. If that is not possible, the seller will want to have extensive collateral securing a promissory note for the purchase price to enable the seller to seize the practice and all of the individual assets of a buyer if the buyer fails to make the required payments.

Tips on Handling Preliminary Negotiations

The early discussions between a buyer and a seller involving the sale of assets or stock can cause problems when the parties do not consult their legal and tax advisers. The veterinarian that you are having the discussions with will want you to commit to various details of the transaction, i.e., what the purchase price will be and how the transaction will be structured. This discussion will almost always occur before you have had your attorney and tax adviser fully analyze the structure of the transaction. It is important that these early discussions be limited to general discussions of the operation of the practice with a focus on providing the potential buyer with information about the practice. Questions about the specifics of the transaction should be deferred until your advisers have fully analyzed the transaction.

You are likely to be viewed in a negative light if you change the terms of your verbal agreement after you have consulted with your lawyer and accountant. However, it is better to be viewed negatively, even if this means that the other party walks away from the transaction, then to agree to bad tax or legal terms.

Due Diligence in a Veterinary Practice Transaction

Due diligence is a thorough examination by the buyer of the seller and his or her assets. It is time consuming, difficult and expensive to conduct. A buyer must determine how much money he or she wants to spend to conduct due diligence and what issues are significant. Where a buyer should spend his or her money varies from transaction to transaction depending upon the circumstances of the seller.

There are two types of due diligence. The first type is the investigation and review conducted during the preliminary discussions. This stage of due diligence is designed to assist the buyer in deciding whether he or she would want to buy the practice if the detailed financial and related information is determined to be accurate. A buyer will frequently bring in a veterinary practice appraiser to assist in negotiating the purchase price based upon the financial information disclosed by the seller. The decisions that the buyer will make at this stage are based upon unsubstantiated information provided by the seller.

The above is in contrast to the due diligence to be conducted after a letter of intent is signed or after the definitive documents are created. At this stage, the buyer is conducting a much more thorough evaluation of certain aspects of the seller's practice to determine if the financial information provided by the seller is accurate and to determine if there are any undisclosed liabilities. A buyer must decide at this stage if he or she will spend the money to have a veterinary practice appraiser conduct a detailed analysis of the practice to determine the accuracy of the financial information disclosed by the seller. This can be an extremely expensive process that is analogous to an audit of the seller's practice. It must be remembered that this is a phase that will never be absolutely complete.

After a buyer has determined how he or she wants to spend his or her due diligence dollars, he or she must decide when the due diligence will be conducted. Buyers need to wait to conduct detailed due diligence until they believe that the principal issues of the transaction have been agreed upon. It is advisable to wait at least until the letter of intent has been signed, but in some transactions it may be safer to wait until a purchase agreement has been finalized. The key for a buyer is to wait until he or she is convinced that the transaction will close, unless he or she finds out that the practice has been misrepresented.

Another factor in determining when a buyer should conduct due diligence is what the schedule is for the transaction. In a perfect transaction, the parties would finalize a letter of intent, finalize the definitive documents, and then have a month or two to complete a buyer's due diligence before closing. However, in most transactions involving veterinary practices, the parties want to close at the same time that the definitive purchase agreement is signed or at a date shortly thereafter.

These rushed schedules make it difficult to conduct necessary due diligence unless the process is started before the parties have finalized the definitive purchase agreements. A buyer would need to have started the process at or near the time that the letter of intent is agreed upon to have been able to conduct any detailed due diligence.

Letter of Intent

After the parties have discussed the transaction in general terms, a letter of intent should be prepared. It does not matter whether the buyer's attorney or the seller's attorney creates the initial draft of the document. However, it is important that both the buyer and the seller seek legal and tax advice on how to structure the transaction prior to finalizing the letter of intent. This is the stage in the transaction when the parties must finalize the structure that they will use to complete the succession plan transaction.

The letter of intent is a mechanism to present to the other party of the structure that you want to utilize in the transaction. All issues that could cause the transaction to fall apart must be addressed and resolved. This should include, but not necessarily be limited to:

- identification of assets or stock involved in transaction
- purchase price or formula for determining purchase price
- method of payment of purchase price
- collateral required to secure promissory note obligation, if any
- tax allocation of purchase price
- post-closing services required of seller
- terms of post-closing agreements, i.e., covenant not-to-compete, employment agreement and stockholders agreement

Letters of intent are not normally structured to be binding upon the parties. It is, however, very important that the letter of intent stage not be approached casually. In 1985, Pennzoil/Texaco/Getty Oil were involved in a lawsuit in which Pennzoil obtained a $10+ billion judgment against Texaco based upon a finding that Texaco had interfered with a "contract" between Pennzoil and the majority shareholders of Getty. Texaco and Getty believed that the discussions that occurred were nothing more then non-binding letters of intent as opposed to a binding contract. Accordingly, it is very important that selling veterinarians be very cautious with their use of letters of intent.

In most associate buy-in structures, parties will want a period of time to determine if they can work together as partners. The goal of the hiring veterinarian is to communicate to the associate that the hiring veterinarian is interested in the associate becoming an owner if the associate works out. However, the hiring veterinarian will not want to spend money on a formalized letter of intent until he or she is convinced that the associate will work out. Accordingly, the letter of intent is very informal and is normally nothing more than language contained within an associate agreement stating the long-term intentions of the parties to have the associate buy an interest in the practice.

LETTER OF INTENT

Pros:
- May make parties feel more comfortable if in writing
- Assures a meeting of the minds by the parties through the expression of purchase price computation
- Prepares parties to consult with legal and tax advisors to determine consequences so that changes can be made or deal canceled without expense of preparation and negotiation of definitive contracts
- Provides format for preparation of definitive documents

Cons:
- May commit a party to a position at an early stage in the negotiation which may be difficult to change later
- May be time-consuming and expensive to negotiate

Contracts in Asset or Stock Transactions

After the letter of intent has been finalized and signed by all parties, the next step involves the preparation of the definitive succession planning transaction documents. The first document that will need to be prepared is the asset or stock purchase agreement.

An agreement for the purchase and sale of a veterinary practice is a complicated document. The agreement must carefully define the positions of both parties to protect them in the event that one party makes misrepresentations or fails to comply with the terms of the agreement. The purchase agreement states all of the details that are necessary to consummate such a transaction.

It is important for a buyer or a seller to keep in mind that attorneys will structure the purchase agreement to benefit their clients' interests. A veterinarian should fight the urge to save money and rely upon the other party's attorney to structure a "fair" contract. It is important that each veterinarian obtain an experienced attorney to represent the veterinarian's interests. A party who is not represented by an experienced attorney will not know whether he or she is getting a fair agreement.

All purchase agreements must contain terms that address the following issues:

Contract Terms Protecting Buyer's
Ownership Interest in Acquired Stock or Assets

Purchase agreements must identify the stock or assets that are being purchased with enough specificity to be able to prove to a court of law that a seller breached. In a stock sale, a purchase agreement must identify in detail the number of shares and the type of shares that are being sold by the seller to the buyer. It is advisable to include the stock certificate number for the shares that are owned by the seller.

In asset purchase transactions, the purchase agreement must clearly identify the categories of assets that are being purchased. Some of the more common descriptions of categories of assets and the unique problems that they pose are as follows:

Inventory

Inventory sales pose an inherent problem because the amount of inventory will fluctuate on a day-to-day basis due to new sales. Two standard techniques are used to properly identify and value inventory for a scheduled closing. First, the parties will jointly conduct an inventory count on the night before the closing to arrive at a final inventory value for closing of the transaction. Second, the parties will place an estimated value on the inventory and will conduct a count on the day of closing. The parties will designate a final settlement date to finalize any credits or debits between the parties based upon the estimated valuation of the inventory that was used for closing. This final settlement date will frequently be scheduled 14 to 90 days after closing.

Furniture, Equipment, Fixtures, Leasehold Improvements, and Instruments

It is important that each of the items in these categories of assets be listed on an attached list. The list should be very detailed and should specify the item, brand, model, and, if possible, the condition of the asset.

A buyer can protect himself from dishonest sellers by taking photographs of the equipment prior to closing. It is not unheard of for a seller to trade out the more valuable equipment that the buyer has been shown with less expensive equipment.

A buyer can also protect himself from purchasing assets that are not in the condition that they appeared to be in by requiring the seller to warrant in the purchase agreement that these assets will be in good working condition at the time of closing. A seller will object to this and request that the purchase agreement reflect that he or she is transferring the assets to the buyer on an "as is" basis. This, however, is always subject to negotiations among the parties.

Supplies

This is another asset category that is subject to abuse by a dishonest seller. It is not unusual for a seller to quit replacing supplies in anticipation of closing on a sale. A buyer can protect him- or herself by making the seller represent in the purchase agreement that the seller will provide the buyer with a normal level of supplies at closing. This contract term will protect a buyer from being forced to purchase thousands of dollars worth of supplies that were not replenished by the seller.

Patient Files and Customer Lists

This important category of assets could also be abused by a dishonest seller. A seller could attempt to mislead a buyer as to the size of the practice by misrepresenting the number of clients served by the practice. This is not as important as some issues because the buyer will also have the financial information of the practice to cross-reference. This problem can be avoided by inserting specific language into the purchase agreement that identifies the approximate number of "active clients." The number of active patients should be narrowly defined to encompass the clients whose pets have been treated in the previous 12 to 24 months of operation.

Contract Rights

This category of assets includes any and all leases, employment agreements, and other contract rights. An example of this is a commercial lease for the practice. It is imperative for a buyer not to lose the rights to the existing office space. If a buyer were to lose a lease immediately or within a couple of years of the sale, the value of the practice would be reduced because the clients would find a closer and more convenient veterinarian. Another example of a contract right is an employment agreement of a key veterinarian employee that prohibits the key employee from competing with the practice.

Goodwill of the Practice

This is a category that includes rights to telephone numbers and rights to trade names and trademarks that have been utilized by the seller. It is important that the purchase agreement contain representations and warranties of the seller warranting the ownership of any trade names or trademarks that the buyer is acquiring.

Accounts Receivable

A purchase agreement must specify if the accounts receivables will be part of the purchase price. If the receivables are not part of the sale, a buyer will want to be permitted to collect the seller's accounts receivables. This is important to a buyer because he or she will not want the clients who have received treatment since the closing to be confused by receiving bills from two different veterinarians. It should be the goal of a buyer to make the transition as smooth as possible for the clients of the practice. The only change that a client should notice is the new veterinarian.

The buyer will normally receive a fee of 5 to 10 percent of the collected receivables for his or her efforts to process the billing for the receivables. The seller will require that his or her receivables be paid in full before the buyer can keep payments from clients that have accounts receivables owing to both the seller and the buyer. A normal receivable agreement will require that the buyer turn over the receivables that are not collected after six months to the seller.

Contract Terms Guaranteeing that Buyer Is Obtaining Good Title to the Assets or Stock

A buyer needs to feel comfortable that he or she is getting title to the assets or stock that he or she is buying. The purchase agreement will require the seller to represent and warrant that the seller owns the assets or stock he or she is selling and that the seller is transferring the assets without any liens or encumbrances. This, however, should not be adequate for a buyer. A buyer of assets, as part of his or her due diligence, needs to conduct a search of the state's uniform commercial code filing records. This will reveal whether the seller has pledged the assets as collateral to secure a loan. If a buyer purchases assets that have been pledged as collateral for a debt, a secured party could take the assets away from the buyer at a later date. This would leave the buyer with no choice but to file a lawsuit against the seller to recover for the buyer's damages. Accordingly, a search must be conducted to confirm that this is not the case.

A purchase agreement in a stock sale will also require a seller to represent and warrant that the buyer is getting good title to the stock. Unfortunately, it is not easy to determine if a seller has good title and the right to sell a stock interest in a corporation. A buyer can, however conduct a careful examination of the corporate records to confirm that the seller properly holds the stock.

It is also important for a buyer to determine if the seller has pledged the stock as security for a loan. Although there is no state agency that records pledges of stock interests, to have an enforceable security interest in stock, a creditor must have possession of the stock certificate. The effect of this is that if the seller has possession of the original stock certificate as recorded on the books of the corporation, there will generally not be a priority security interest to cause the buyer to lose the stock that he or she is purchasing.

Contract Terms to Protect a Buyer from Liabilities of a Seller

Asset purchase agreements commonly identify what liabilities, if any, that a buyer agrees to assume and become obligated to pay as part of the transaction. It is extremely important that a buyer take the necessary steps to avoid being subject to liabilities of the seller that the buyer did not agree to assume as part of the transaction.

A buyer insulates his or her practice from the liabilities of the seller by complying with each state's laws regarding successor entity liability. Many state laws do not insulate a non-ordinary course buyer of assets unless it complies with the state's bulk sale transfer law. Compliance with most state bulk sales transfer acts involves the following:

✓ Require seller to furnish a list of its business creditors to buyer
✓ Compile a list of the specific assets being transferred
✓ Give proper notice of the sale of the assets to the seller's business creditors
✓ Make arrangements to assure payment of seller's creditors from the proceeds of the sale
✓ Buyer keeping a list of creditors and assets after the transfer and making them available for inspection and copying by the seller's creditors

Many states have done away with their bulk sale transfer acts and have established different standards to insulate a buying practice from liabilities of a selling practice. In these states, buyers no longer need to comply with the specific notice provisions of the bulk sales transfer act. The primary requirement under these states laws is that the transaction between the seller and buyer be an "arms length" transaction where the buyer has given the seller "reasonable equivalent value in good faith." If this standard is met, the buyer will not be liable to the creditors of the seller that the buyer did not agree to pay.

Contract Terms for Purchase Price and Payment Terms

The purchase agreement must specify the purchase price, plus the formula, if any, for determining the additional purchase price of the inventory. If inventory is to be valued after the closing, the purchase agreement must specify the date that the additional purchase price of the inventory will be determined.

The purchase agreement must identify how the purchase price will be paid at closing. The purchase agreement must identify the amount that will be paid as earnest money, the amount to be paid at closing in cash or certified funds, and the amount to be paid in the form of a promissory note.

The purchase agreement must identify the terms of the promissory note. It must state the amount, the annual interest rate, and the payment term. The purchase agreement must also state whether the promissory note can be prepaid. Frequently, a seller will not want a buyer to have the right to prepay a promissory note in order to spread the gain to the seller over a number of years. A seller may also want to prohibit a buyer from prepaying in order to receive the negotiated interest rate for the term of the promissory note. The interest rate on the promissory note will frequently be higher than the seller can receive in other investments at what the seller may perceive is a less risky investment. The buyer, on the other hand, will want the ability to prepay a promissory note in order to maximize his or her options. A buyer does not want to be prohibited from prepaying the promissory note if he or she decides to sell the practice before the end of the payment term.

The purchase agreement should also identify the collateral that the buyer has agreed to pledge to secure the promissory note obligation. A buyer will always be required to pledge the stock or the assets being purchased as part of the transaction. There are unusual circumstances, however, where a buyer has paid the majority of the purchase price by obtaining a loan from a third party. In this circumstance, a seller may be convinced to subordinate first position on the assets or stock being sold to the other lender in order to obtain payment at closing of the majority of the purchase price. The effect of the seller subordinating his or her position as priority secured creditor is that the seller's security interest is then second position to the priority secured creditor. If the buyer defaults, the seller will not be able to take the stock or assets back from the buyer unless there is enough value in the assets to pay off the priority secured party and the seller. This is unlikely in most transactions. The seller may be willing to take this risk, however, because of the amount of the purchase price that was paid at closing.

A seller will want additional collateral to secure a promissory note of a buyer. The seller will require that the individual veterinarian and his or her spouse personally guarantee the promissory note obligation. The personal guarantee is only necessary if the buyer is taking title as a corporation or a limited liability company as opposed to it being necessary because a buyer is individually responsible for a promissory note that he or she signs as a sole proprietorship.

A buyer should also expect the seller to require that the buyer obtain life insurance and disability insurance to secure the promissory note payments in the event that the buyer dies or becomes disabled.

Tax Allocation Contract Terms

A purchase agreement will also identify a tax allocation for the purchase price when the transaction involves an asset sale or the sale of "S" corporation stock. The tax allocation is very important to both the buyer and the seller because it can control how the gain is taxed for the seller and how the purchase price is depreciated for the buyer. A tax allocation may also have a bearing on the amount of the local transfer or use tax as a result of the transaction.

Contract Terms Identifying Contingencies to Transaction Being Completed

It is important for a buyer that the purchase agreement identify circumstances that will permit him or her to back out of the transaction without a penalty. A buyer will want a right to back out of a transaction if the seller cannot obtain permission from a commercial landlord to assign the lease to the buyer. This is significant to a buyer because the value of the practice is affected if the buyer cannot practice in the existing offices. Under most commercial leases, a tenant is in default if he or she assigns a lease to a third party without receiving permission from the landlord. Accordingly, a buyer does not want to be obligated to buy a practice unless he or she gets permission to take over the commercial lease. It is also important for a buyer to have the right to get out of the transaction if, as a result of due diligence, he or she becomes uncomfortable about the practice. Another reason to have a contingency to back out of the transaction is if the buyer is unable to secure outside financing for some, if not all, of the purchase price.

Contract Warranties and Representations

The parties to a purchase agreement will be required to make certain warranties and representations. These warranties and representations will vary depending upon the transaction and the skill of the attorneys involved, but they are very important because they are the primary legal recourse for a buyer when a seller has made misrepresentations about the practice. An example of this involves a very simple contract clause regarding the accuracy of the seller's financial records that states that "the financial statements provided as part of this transaction fully and accurately describe the assets and liabilities of the seller as of the date thereof." If, after the closing, a buyer determines that the financial statements did not "... fully and accurately describe the assets and liabilities ..." a buyer will have a claim against the seller.

A seller will try to minimize the risk that an error in his or her financial statements will lead to a claim by renegotiating the language of the warranty and representation. The buyer will try to negotiate a change to this representation and warranty to reflect that the financial statements are accurate "to the best of the seller's knowledge." A buyer that agrees to such a change is taking a very big risk. If, after the closing, the buyer determines that the seller's financial statements were not accurate, the buyer will have to prove not only that the statements were inaccurate but also that the seller knew that the statements were inaccurate. This is a much more difficult standard.

Warranties and representations can be manipulated by a dishonest seller to work in the seller's favor. A dishonest seller could work with an accountant who puts together inaccurate financial statements. The seller could then claim that he or she had no knowledge that the financial statements were inaccurate because the accountant did all of the work and the seller believed that the statements were accurate.

Veterinarians who choose not to spend the money to conduct a thorough due diligence must have well-drafted warranty and representation contract terms to protect them in the event that the financials turn out to be inaccurate.

Contract Terms Covering
Disputes between the Buyer and the Seller

It is important that a purchase agreement contain mandatory binding arbitration provisions for disputes. A binding arbitration provision will expedite the resolution of any dispute and substantially reduce the cost of litigating the matter. The principal reason that the costs will be reduced is because in an arbitrated proceeding, discovery is kept to a minimum. In addition, an arbitrated proceeding will go to hearing much quicker than a court proceeding.

The purchase agreement should permit a buyer to go to court if the buyer wants to enforce a covenant not to compete. A buyer must be careful to ensure that the binding arbitration language of the purchase agreement does not prevent him or her from obtaining an injunction from a court. A court has the ability to rule on an injunction on an expedited basis while an arbitrator does not.

It is also important that a purchase agreement provide that the successful party in a dispute be entitled to recover his or her attorney's fees. This can have the effect of influencing a party that has acted improperly to resolve the dispute as opposed to litigating the matter.

Contracts to Implement the
Transfers under the Purchase Agreement

Every veterinary practice purchase agreement will require that the parties enter into additional agreements to implement their respective obligations. These agreements include: bills of sale; assignment and assumption agreements; promissory notes; security agreements; and covenant not-to-compete agreements. It is very important that these documents are drafted to be consistent with the obligations identified in the purchase agreement.

Bill of Sale

A bill of sale is a document transferring legal title to a buyer from a seller. Frequently, it will identify the type of warranty, if any, for the condition of the assets.

Assignment Agreement/Assumption Agreement

These agreements will transfer rights and liabilities of a seller to a buyer. Examples of this include commercial office space leases, equipment leases, and employment agreements of key non-owner veterinarians.

A seller will want to be released from any liability on an assumed obligation after the closing of the transaction. A lessor, however, has little motivation to let a seller off the hook. It is always subject to negotiation, but sellers will frequently be obligated if the buyer defaults on these obligations. The purchase agreement will require that the buyer indemnify the seller if the buyer defaults on one of these obligations. Unfortunately, if the buyer is not making the payments on these assumed debts, he or she is not likely to be making payments to the seller for the purchase price. Accordingly, the seller would be unlikely to be able to recover for his or her liability to an assumed obligation.

Promissory Note

The promissory note is the legal document that the buyer signs at closing to formalize the seller's financing of all or part of the purchase price. The promissory note will identify the amount that the buyer is borrowing from the seller as well as the annual interest rate and the term for payment.

The promissory note will also identify the collateral that the buyer is pledging to secure the promissory note obligation.

It is important that a buyer require that the promissory note contain language permitting him or her to offset the monthly payments if the seller misrepresented the practice, thereby causing the buyer damages. This can include debts that the buyer was forced to pay on behalf of the seller or damages arising from misrepresentations regarding the practice. This is an important contract term because if the buyer does not have this right to offset the monthly promissory note payment, he or she would be forced to continue to make monthly promissory note payments while suing the seller for misrepresenting the practice. The reason for this is that a promissory note is a separate obligation from the purchase agreement. A buyer is not legally entitled to quit making payments on the promissory note without language authorizing an offset.

Security Agreements

The goal of a seller is to position himself to take the practice back if the buyer defaults. In order to have the legal right to seize the assets, the seller must have a perfected security interest. Security agreements are the legal documents that formalize the buyer's pledging of collateral to secure the promissory note obligation. It is this document, combined with the filing of certain documents with state and county offices, that permits the seller to seize the practice in the event that the buyer defaults on his or her obligations.

Each category of collateral requires different contract terms in order for the seller to obtain a perfected security interest. An example of this is a buyer who pledges his or her stock interest in his or her practice to secure the purchase price promissory note. In order for the seller to have a perfected security interest in the stock, the seller must hold the stock certificate pursuant to the terms of a pledge agreement.

Seller's Agreement Not to Compete or Solicit

It is important for a buyer of a veterinary practice to be protected against a seller setting up a practice that will compete with the buyer or solicit the clients of the buyer's practice. Under most state laws, there is no protection for a buyer unless a valid covenant not to compete is entered into with the seller as part of the purchase transaction.

To be enforceable under most state laws, the covenant not-to-compete agreement must be reasonable in geographic scope and length of time. What is reasonable varies from state to state and varies depending upon the specific circumstances of the practice.

It is important that a buyer be advised of how courts in the buyer's state have enforced these covenants. In some states, judges who rule that a covenant-not-to-compete agreement is unreasonable are permitted to judicially modify the terms of the covenant and redraft the geographic scope or reduce the length of time for the covenant. If you are a buyer in such a state, you can afford to be aggressive and insert a geographic area and a length of time that is at risk of being unreasonable. If a judge does rewrite the terms of the covenant-not-to-compete agreement, a buyer still has the protection of the covenant on the terms that the judge specified. The only risk for a buyer is the cost of litigating the issue.

This is in sharp contrast to states that require a judge to void a covenant-not-to-compete agreement if its terms are deemed unreasonable. If you are a buyer of a practice in that state, you will need to be conservative and only designate a geographic area and length of time that will be enforced by a judge.

A buyer should also make sure that the covenant-not-to-compete agreement prohibits a seller from soliciting the client base. Covenant-not-to-compete agreements only serve to keep a selling veterinarian from opening a practice within a specific geographic area; they do not prevent a seller from soliciting the client base to be treated at the seller's new practice outside of the covenant-not-to-compete agreement area.

A trap for a buyer of a veterinary practice is that the seller of the practice may not be the only person who needs to be bound by the terms of a covenant-not-to-compete agreement. A buyer should be careful to make sure that all treating veterinarians who were employed by the selling veterinarian are prohibited from soliciting the client base and competing with the practice. An employee of the practice is not legally bound by the terms of the non-compete agreement signed by the seller. A buying veterinarian can protect him- or herself by requiring the seller to convince his or her employee veterinarians to enter into enforceable employment agreements with the practice that prohibit them from soliciting or competing with the practice.

A buyer should not agree to buy the practice without such protection. Frequently, the value of the practice will be dependent upon keeping key veterinarian employees from soliciting or competing with the practice. In most states it is advisable that the buyer require the selling veterinarian to pay the employee veterinarian a sum of money to make the non-compete and non-solicitation terms enforceable.

Certain contractual terms can protect a seller of a practice in the event that the buyer fails to comply with his or her obligations. A seller should require that the covenant not to compete be void upon the default of the buyer. This is important to permit a seller to step back into the practice under a default scenario. A court would probably not enforce a covenant not to compete against a seller who had to take back a practice, but it is good to have the contractual language to avoid an adverse ruling.

Another provision to protect a seller is a reverse covenant not to compete against the buyer in the event of a default by the buyer. This will prevent a buyer from losing the practice after he or she fails to make the payments and opening a practice down the street. The value of the practice in a resale situation will be greatly reduced if a new buyer cannot be convinced that the former buyer is legally prevented from competing or soliciting the practice. This reverse covenant not to compete can also be assigned to a new buyer to give the buyer the right to protect his or her practice.

Contracts between the Owners of Veterinary Practices

It is important that the owners of a veterinary practice formalize the terms of their relationship. There are two basic types of contracts: contracts between an owner/employee and the practice for services rendered; and contracts between owners.

Ownership Employment/Compensation Agreements

Veterinary practice owners must have agreements governing their compensation for services rendered to the practice. These compensation agreements can be structured as separate employment agreements with the practice or can be tied together as part of an agreement between the owners.

There are two basic structures for owner compensation for services rendered. The compensation can be based on either the production of the individual veterinarian or on ownership interest. These two structures, however, have numerous variations that can be used to customize the structure to the needs of the practice and the owners.

The benefit to a production-based compensation structure is that the veterinarians are encouraged to work harder by being paid more if they produce more. This production-based structure also has the benefit of minimizing problems between owners when one veterinarian takes more time off than the other.

It is important that the employment agreement with the practice contain non-competition/non-solicitation terms. If an owner is not limited by non-competition/non-solicitation terms, the practice is subject to being harmed should the owner leave the practice. This protection goes beyond the normal protections provided to owners in a stockholder's agreement.

Stockholder Agreements

The principal objective of a stockholder agreement is to restrict the transfer of the ownership interest in the practice. There are two types of restrictions that are created in stockholder agreements: provisions to prevent the sale of an ownership interest and provisions to require the sale of an ownership interest.

These restrictions on the transfer of ownership interests are especially important to minority interest holders. Minority interest holders could suffer greatly if majority interest holders were allowed to sell their shares and the associated control of the practice was sold to an outsider who is not sympathetic to the minority interest holders' concerns. Similarly, majority shareholders may suffer from the sale of even one share to a recalcitrant, argumentative shareholder, particularly in a veterinary practice where the owners must work closely together to make the practice a success.

There are a variety of triggering events commonly used to force or prevent a buyout. One of these triggering events involves a selling owner who has received a good faith offer to purchase his or her interest. It is important that the shareholder's agreement define what a "good faith offer" is in order to prevent a selling owner from trying to avoid the terms of the agreement by falsely claiming that a good faith offer exists.

Another common triggering event to force a sale of ownership interest is the death or permanent disability of an owner. A stockholder's agreement can be very beneficial to both the family of an owner who dies or becomes disabled and the remaining owners. A disabled owner or the family of an owner who dies receives the benefit of having a market created for the sale of the ownership interest. The remaining owners of the practice also benefit because they are permitted to control who will buy the ownership interest.

There are other triggering events, as well, that are beneficial to a veterinary practice. The retirement of a veterinarian, for example, is a common triggering event. This provision can be open-ended to be effective whenever an owner wants to retire from the practice of veterinary medicine, or it can require the owner to be a certain age or have practiced for a certain period of time with the practice. This is an important provision for implementation of a selling veterinarian's succession plan.

Another triggering event occurs when the owner is terminated from employment with the practice. This commonly occurs when there is an employment agreement identifying grounds for termination. If no employment agreement exists, it is common to include a provision in the stockholder agreement that it is a triggering event when an owner fails to maintain his or her professional license or to maintain his or her production at a certain level or work a set number of hours in a set period. This provision will give the practice the ability to get rid of an owner who is no longer focused on the success of the practice or is no longer able to practice.

The owners must also decide under what circumstances they want the remaining owners to be forced to buy out an owner's interest as opposed to their giving the remaining owners the option to buy out an owner's interest. Stockholder agreements are frequently structured to force the purchase of an owner's interest upon the death, disability, or retirement of any owner. There are other circumstances such as termination of employment and receipt of a good faith offer where the remaining owners may only want to be provided with the option to buy. Stockholder agreements that require that the remaining owners be provided with an option to purchase are normally permitted to sell to a qualified third party if the remaining owners fail to exercise their option to buy the ownership interest.

It is normally advisable to structure the option to require the seller to offer the stock option first to the corporation and then to the remaining stockholders. This will maximize the options for the remaining owners to structure a buy-out in the most favorable manner.

A choice must be made at the drafting stage between a restriction permitting a partial purchase of the offered stock or one requiring a purchase of all-or-nothing by the corporation or the shareholders. A seller of the stock is at a definite disadvantage if the remaining shareholders are permitted to only buy a small percentage of the seller's stock. A seller who has received a good faith offer to sell the stock is likely to lose the buyer if less than all of his or her stock is available. In addition, a seller will be discouraged from selling his or her interest if he or she could be left with a partial share of the stock. This may, however, be the desired drafting approach if the goal is to prevent an owner from selling his or her ownership interest. In the spirit of fairness, it is a better approach to require that the entire ownership interest be bought or none at all. The ownership interest could still be purchased by a combination of the corporation and the remaining owners but with the requirement that it be a combined all-or-none proposition.

It is important that the owners agree upon a value or a formula to value the ownership interest in the practice in the event that a triggering event occurs. An advisable approach is to designate a per share value for a set period of time, i.e., 12 or 24 months. The agreement should then provide that after the designated value term expires, a specific formula be used to value the practice. There are a variety of formulas that can be used to value a practice. If the owners designate a specific formula, it is important that they fully understand the effect of their selection.

Another option is for the owners to designate a specific appraiser to conduct the appraisal as opposed to a specific formula. If the parties do not wish to designate a specific appraiser, provisions should be made for the selection of an appraiser in the event that the parties cannot agree.

The stockholders agreement should state how the purchase of the ownership interest will be funded. It is advisable, although not required, that insurance be obtained to fund buy-outs arising from death or disability. There are various options available to a practice and its owners that should be explored to maximize the tax benefits for the purchase and ownership of insurance to fund a buy-out.

The stockholders agreement should also identify the terms for installment payment if there are no insurance proceeds available for a buy-out. The focus of the owners should be to balance the desire of the seller to get paid as quickly as possible with the desire of the remaining owners to continue to operate the practice while paying off the debt.

Solo Group Practice or Practice Affiliation: Is It Right for You?

6

Group Practice or Practice Affiliation

Setting up and operating a veterinary practice is more expensive today than it has ever been before. It can cost hundreds of thousands of dollars to set up a practice with updated equipment.

A compounding factor in the current economics of veterinary medicine is the narrow profit margins in the industry. In most markets, veterinarians undercut their prices for core services in order to compete with large national chains. This has created an economic environment that is squeezing profit margins and making it more and more difficult to obtain the necessary profitability.

These economic realities have a bearing on any capital purchase by a veterinarian. Any veterinarian interested in opening a practice or updating his or her equipment or facilities must evaluate all of his or her options to avoid suffocating under the debt that could be incurred. Historically, the preferred option by veterinarians who cannot afford to acquire updated equipment or facilities has been to enter into a partnership or co-ownership with one or more veterinarians. This option permits the veterinarian to purchase the equipment and update his or her facilities with the combined resources and economy to scale to make it cost effective. Unfortunately, this approach also brings problems inherent in co-ownership of a veterinary practice.

A multitude of issues can and frequently do arise when a practice has more than one owner. Some of the more problematic areas for co-owners are: the sharing of profits and losses (this is especially evident when the veterinarians do not share similar work habits); division of new clients; spending habits; and staff management issues. Veterinarians frequently avoid co-ownership relationships because of these problems.

The concept of "practice affiliation," or "solo group practice," is a viable alternative to a traditional partnership or other forms of co-ownership. The terms "practice affiliation" and "solo group practice" can be defined as an association of two or more veterinarians, each owning an undivided interest in the veterinary facility for the sole purpose of sharing the facility and overhead expenses, while retaining separate, independent practices.

The concept of "practice affiliation," or "solo group practice," is an approach to the operation of a veterinary practice that provides the economic benefits of a multiple veterinarian-owned practice with separate and distinct practice ownership. In its most simplistic form, it is a sharing of office space and equipment to minimize the expenses of operating the practice. In a more complex structure, it can be very similar to a partnership or joint ownership relationship.

Except in the most simplistic of structures, a solo group, or practice affiliation, needs to be structured as a separate legal entity, with the individual veterinary practices or individual veterinarians being the owners of the new entity. This is very important if the solo group markets the group under a name separate from the names of the individual veterinary practices. The marketing of a trade name is very expensive, and the solo group needs to take the necessary steps to protect its rights to this name.

It is also important to have the solo group operate as a separate legal entity for liability purposes. The goal should be to insulate the individual practices from lawsuits arising from actions of the other veterinarians. As was discussed in Chapter 4, certain legal entities provide the owners of an entity with insulation from the liabilities of the entity. If the solo group is not formed as an entity that insulates the individual owners, the individual veterinarians could be named as parties to a lawsuit as a result of actions of one of the other veterinarians. The legal documents created for the solo group would attempt to provide a defense to such a claim; however, the individual veterinarians would be forced to defend the litigation.

A creditor who chooses to name all of the individual veterinarians in a lawsuit will claim that the solo group is a general partnership or a joint venture. Such a claim will provide the creditor with the legal authority to name the owners in the lawsuit because individual owners are liable for the entire debt of a general partnership or joint venture. This could be avoided if the legal entity is a limited liability company, limited liability partnership, or a corporation where the individual owners have a shield from liability. Accordingly, it is important that the veterinarians protect themselves through the formation of an appropriate legal entity.

SOLO GROUP PRACTICE OR PRACTICE AFFILIATION

Pros: • Allows for separate ownership of practices
• Offers affordable acquisition of equipment and facilities

Cons: • Results in loss of control over autonomous operations
• Requires sharing of management of employees

All Solo Group Practices, or Practice Affiliations, Should Have a Written Agreement

Although any important verbal agreement should be in writing, it is especially important that this be the case in a solo group practice or a practice affiliation. Significant legal issues involving the legal relationship between the veterinarians need to be addressed in a written solo group practice, or practice affiliation, agreement. These contract terms could ultimately save a veterinarian thousands of dollars in defense of a lawsuit that is focused on the actions of one of the other veterinary practices within the solo group practice, or practice affiliation.

The form of the agreement will vary depending upon the type of legal entity that is created to operate the solo group. If the solo group is of a very simplistic form, the agreement between the parties will be of more significance because of the need for individual veterinarians to be protected from liabilities arising from actions of the other veterinarians. If the solo group legal entity is of a form that will provide insulation from liability for the individual veterinarians, there are other issues between the individual veterinarians that remain very significant.

Some of the major terms that need to be included in a solo group practice, or practice affiliation, agreement are as follows:

Statement as to Separate Ownership of Veterinarians' Practices

This could be the most important term of the agreement. It must be made very clear in the agreement that the veterinary practices are separately owned and that the practices are not partners, joint ventures, employees, or independent contractors. This is significant because the veterinarians in the practice need to be able to prove to a court of law that they are were not partners or joint ventures with the other veterinarians if a lawsuit for malpractice is filed. If a court was to find that the veterinarians were partners or joint ventures, the veterinarians could be forced to pay for the liability of one of the other veterinarians.

Statement as to Facility Ownership

The solo group agreement needs to reflect the ownership of the commercial office facility. One of the first decisions that should be made when forming a solo group is whether the owners of the solo group need to obtain a new commercial office facility or if the existing facility of one of the veterinarians is adequate. If one of the existing veterinarians' office space is adequate, the solo group must decide whether the group will obtain a new lease or will sublease from the existing tenant. If the solo group desires to sublease, the existing tenant will be required to obtain written permission from his or her landlord.

The solo group agreement should require that the solo group veterinarians personally guarantee any facility obligation of the solo group. The landlord is also likely to require a personal guarantee of the lease obligations from all of the veterinarians in the solo group.

If the solo group is subleasing the existing facility of one of the veterinarians, the solo group needs to address the payment of the value of the leasehold improvements to the existing tenant. This will be in the form of a buy-in to the solo group operation to cover the startup operation expenses.

Identification of Solo Group Assets and
Statement as to Percentage of Ownership

A solo group practice or practice affiliation agreement must contain language specifying what assets are owned by the solo group and the percentage of ownership of each veterinarian. Such a contract term is important because a creditor who obtains a judgment against one of the veterinary practices in the solo group may attempt to collect or execute on the judgment by seizing the assets of the solo group. This would be an impermissible execution under most states' laws because the veterinary practice that is obligated on the judgment only owns an undivided interest in the assets. This is not to say that the creditor could not ultimately seize the interest in the assets that the veterinarian owned, but it would prevent the creditor from actually seizing the asset and forcing it to be sold. It is important to keep in mind that you cannot prevent a creditor from naming your veterinary practice as a defendant in a lawsuit; however, if the solo group practice agreement clearly identifies the ownership of the solo group assets and the percentages of ownership, you have provided your litigation attorney with the ammunition to defend your interests.

Statement as to Assets Owned by Individual Veterinarians

A solo group practice agreement must contain language specifying what assets are owned individually by the veterinarians. Most solo group practices will have certain assets that are owned by individual veterinarians but are used by the entire solo group.

Term of Agreement

The solo group practice agreement must identify a starting and an ending point. A standard termination date is at the end of the lease term. However, these contract terms are frequently drafted to permit a solo group to automatically renew the agreement for a certain agreed-upon number of years. Later in this chapter, contract terms identifying events that cause termination of a specific veterinarian's ownership interest or the termination of the solo group will be discussed.

Name Ownership

It is important that the agreement clearly indicate that each veterinary practice owns all rights and interest to their own corporate and trade names. The solo group contract will provide, however, that the solo group practice has the right to adopt a common trade name for the operation of the solo group.

Management Structure

The solo group agreement must provide for a management structure for the solo group. The type and complexity of the structure will depend upon the size and needs of the group. A simple structure may provide for each veterinarian to have one vote with a majority vote controlling day-to-day management issues. This type of management structure normally requires a higher percentage of the veterinarians to approve capital purchases, leases, and other significant financial issues. The effectiveness of the management structure adopted by a solo group will have a lot to do with the ultimate success of the group. Differing opinions as to how a solo group is managed will always exist, and it is important that the management structure provide the flexibility for the solo group to change as its needs change.

Financial Responsibilities of the Veterinarians of the Solo Group

The solo group agreement must identify the rights and responsibilities of each veterinarian as they relate to expenses of the solo group. It is extremely important that the solo group agreement clearly identify a formula for determining the obligations of each veterinarian in the group. The formula for determining the amount or percentage of the solo group expense that must be paid by each veterinarian varies from group to group. It is, however, frequently structured based upon fixed operational expenses and variable individual expenses. Some of the expenses that the solo group agreement must identify a formula for dividing are the following:

- Office Facility Expenses:
  - ✓ rent
  - ✓ utilities
  - ✓ additional rent and expenses under the commercial lease

- Maintenance and Repair Expenses:
  - ✓ equipment owned by solo group
  - ✓ equipment individually owned by the owners
  - ✓ veterinary supplies
  - ✓ office supplies
  - ✓ fixed office expenses
  - ✓ variable office expenses

Rights to Use of Facility of Solo Group

The solo group agreement needs to address the use of the solo group facility. The solo group agreement should specify what areas of the facility will be exclusive areas for each individual veterinarian and his or her staff and which areas will be common. The solo group agreement also needs to specify how the common areas will be used from an operational standpoint. The agreement should also address whether exclusive areas of the facility can be used for emergencies and, if so, it should identify what is considered an acceptable emergency.

Sharing and Compensation of Staff

The parties need to agree on the staff that will be hired by the solo group. If the group chooses to not have its own staff, the agreement should address how each veterinarian's staff will be shared and compensated.

Termination of Solo Group

It is important that the parties agree on the circumstances when the solo group will terminate a membership of one of the solo group members. There are several triggering events that normally control the termination of solo group members. Some of the more common provisions are: 1) death; 2) disability; and 3) default under solo group agreement.

Buy-Sell Agreement

In some of the more complicated solo group structures, the solo groups are operated in much the same fashion as group-owned veterinary practices. In these solo groups, the members will frequently want contract terms to permit the individual veterinarians to buy the other veterinarians' practices under certain triggering events. The most common triggering events giving rise to the option to purchase one of the veterinarians' practices are death or disability of the owner and a bonafide offer to sell from a third party. These contract terms will permit the continuation of the solo group regardless of the ownership of the individual veterinary practices.

These contract provisions will also identify a formula that will be used to value the practices and the payment terms for payment of the option price.

Mutual Indemnification and Hold Harmless

The solo group agreement must require the individuals to indemnify the other veterinarians in the event they incur expenses as a result of the actions of one of the other veterinarians. The agreement must also specifically require the veterinarians to hold harmless the other veterinarians and provide a defense for any litigation that may arise as a result of their actions. Assuming the obligated veterinarian is financially viable, this type of contract term will protect a veterinarian who is sued simply because he or she is a member of a solo group.

Prohibition of Solicitation and Covenants Not to Compete

It will be extremely important that the solo group agreement contain provisions prohibiting the veterinarians from solicitation of the other veterinarians' clients. It will also be important to require the veterinarians to enter into a non-compete agreement with the solo group to prevent their setting up a practice in an area surrounding the solo group if they were to separate from the group.

Allocation of New Clients

If the solo group owns its own telephone number and markets the solo group, it will need to establish a policy and procedure for allocating new clients among its members.

Ownership of Telephone Number

If the solo group obtains and markets its own telephone number, the solo group agreement must address the ownership of the solo group number to avoid any claims for the telephone number after a veterinarian separates from the solo group. This will not be an issue if each veterinarian maintains his or her own telephone number and marketing.

Ownership of Client and Patient Records

The solo group agreement must address the ownership of client and patient records to avoid any claims for client and patient records after a veterinarian separates from the solo group.

Additional Concerns for Veterinarians Entering into Solo Group Practices

The decision to enter into a solo group has long-term implications to a veterinary practice. A veterinarian should not enter into a solo group without fully understanding the effect of the decision. Entering into a solo group is, however, an opportunity for a veterinarian to obtain facilities, equipment, and a structure that can benefit his or her practice.

The Effect of a Solo Group Structure for General and Specialty Practices

A solo group practice is especially effective and beneficial when it is a combination of specialty practices. Frequently, good cross-marketing of the various specialty practices results. In addition, there is a limited risk in this type of structure that veterinarians within the solo group will take clients from other veterinarians within the solo group.

General practice veterinarians are often more concerned about entering into such a structure because of the increased risk of theft of clients. In general veterinary practices, there is more of a risk of theft of clients because the veterinarians generally provide the same services to the same types of clients. There are of course differences between small and large animal practices, but most of the time, solo groups involving general veterinary practices combine similar veterinary practices.

How can a general practice veterinarian feel comfortable about entering into a solo group structure with this increased risk? The veterinarian must enter into this type of structure possessing a comfort level for the honesty of the other veterinarians. It is not advisable for a general practice veterinarian to enter into such a structure if he or she doesn't have a comfortable relationship with the other veterinarians.

The solo group agreement must be well drafted to protect the veterinarians' ownership interests in their client records and patient files. The veterinarian must feel confident that he or she has a legal recourse in the event of a breach by a solo group veterinarian.

How effective is it to combine specialty veterinary practices with general veterinary practices? This is an issue that needs to be approached with caution by a specialty practice. Specialty practices survive based on referrals by general veterinary practitioners. A specialty practices referring veterinarians may become uncomfortable if the specialist that they are referring their clients to has a general practitioner within their solo group. They could be concerned that they would lose their client to the general practice that operates within the solo group.

If this was to happen to any great extent, a specialty practice could actually be harmed by being involved in the solo group. It is important that a specialty practice consider this factor when entering into a solo group composed of specialty and general veterinary practices.

A Solo Group Can Be Adversely Impacted by a New Practice with a Tax-Qualified Retirement Plan

Many veterinary practices establish a tax-qualified retirement plan as an employee benefit. However, for many of these practices the retirement plan has been adopted to maximize the benefits to the owners. This is accomplished by the owners adopting a retirement plan with strict criteria that limit when an employee is eligible to participate. This can permit an individual owner to limit his or her obligation or liability to make contributions to the retirement plan and target the retirement plan to benefit himself. The criteria that are normally utilized by an owner to limit the number of employees who can participate are based upon age, years of employment, and extended vesting terms.

This attempt to funnel the benefits to the owner is limited by nondiscrimination rules that establish tests that an employer must meet before he or she can distribute a larger percentage of the retirement plan benefits to her- or himself and other highly compensated employees. As a result of these non-discrimination rules, it frequently benefits veterinary practices to keep their staffs small in order to maximize the benefits to the owners and the other highly compensated employees.

A problem arises when an individual veterinary practice with a tax-qualified retirement plan joins a solo group. The Internal Revenue Service has rules that prevent owners from establishing multiple legal entities to evade the non-discrimination rules aimed at preventing the owners from funneling more of the benefits to themselves. As a result of these Internal Revenue Service requirements, before a solo group is formed, the individual practices must analyze the legal effect of forming a solo group if one or more of the individual practices have tax-qualified retirement plans.

Legal Relationships with Associate Veterinarians

7

You have been analyzing your options to structure a succession plan to exit your practice for a couple of years. During this period of time, your practice has been getting busier and busier. From time to time you think about hiring an additional associate, or if a sole-doctor practice, your first associate. Then one day, unexpectedly, you are introduced to someone who appears to be a perfect associate candidate for your practice. You immediately picture yourself being able to spend more time with your family or on the golf course. You also consider the benefits of structuring a succession plan, with the new associate buying out your interest in the practice. After several interviews and considerable thought, you decide that you will hire this person as your associate. After all, what do you have to lose?

All Associate Agreements Should Be in Writing

It is a good business practice to reduce any important verbal agreement to writing. An associate agreement is no exception and should be written and signed by both parties. This is true whether the associate is classified as an employee or an independent contractor.

All too frequently veterinarians tell me that the doctor they work for or the associate they want to hire is a man of his word. They claim that it is unnecessary to have a written agreement because both are honest and honorable individuals and a written agreement complicates a straightforward relationship. The flaw in this logic is that two people will frequently interpret and remember different details from a verbal conversation. If you ask two perfectly honest individuals about the specific terms of an agreement that arose after a verbal conversation, each one will focus on certain details that will frequently conflict with the understanding or memory of the other individual.

This problem can become serious if it involves terms of a verbal associate agreement that relate to compensation or other significant issues. When this happens, the party who feels that he or she has been misled (normally the associate) may start questioning whether the hiring veterinarian is honest or is trying to take advantage of him or her. The effect of such a scenario is that the parties who once believed each other to be honest begin questioning each other's character. This is especially unfortunate if the doctors work well together otherwise and are looking for a long-term business relationship.

This problem can easily be avoided by having a well-drafted associate agreement or independent contractor agreement. A poorly drafted agreement that fails to address important issues is frequently no better than a verbal agreement because a misunderstanding or ambiguity on important issues remains. It is also important to understand that ambiguities in written agreements are construed against the drafters of the agreements. The effect of this is that the party who drafts the agreement, frequently the hiring veterinarian, will have any ambiguous or missing sections construed against his or her own legal interest and for the legal interest of the associate. The legal system has evolved over hundreds of years to protect the weak by construing the ambiguous contract provisions against the drafter.

Some of the major terms relating to business issues that should be included in a written associate agreement are as follows:

Definition of Associate as an Employee

Make it clear in the agreement that the associate is your employee and not an independent contractor. This language is important to avoid any confusion as to the intentions of the parties. However, if your practice is audited, the IRS will use its own tests to determine whether or not the associate is in fact an employee or independent contractor.

Length of Term

When does the associate's employment begin and when does it end? Most agreements provide that they can be terminated by either party and for any reason upon either 30, 60 or 90 days' notice to the other party. In addition, you need to address what happens upon the associate's death or disability, loss of license, or other circumstances.

Duties and Hours

Define the associate's work schedule and the associate's duties and responsibilities. The practice should have a very broad and flexible definition of duties to avoid an associate's narrowing the scope of his or her job duties. There needs to be language permitting the practice to alter the specific tasks that are being undertaken by the associate so long as it falls within the broad definition in the associate agreement.

The associate agreement should generally permit a practice to alter the hours of work by the associate, i.e., emergencies, on call, etc.

Does the associate have the right to work in other practices? The associate agreement should specifically indicate whether the associate is permitted to work in other practices.

Compensation

What compensation will you pay the associate: fixed monthly, hourly rate, percentage of collection, percentage of production, or a combination? What is the going rate for associate salaries? While it is important to know what associates are being paid in the marketplace to determine a fair compensation, it is more important to know what you can afford to pay an associate. A proper analysis of your practice income, expenses, and projections is in order. The practice should also consider sharing this information with the associate if the associate has expectations of a big raise that the practice cannot afford. If your practice cannot afford to give a large raise, you will have to decide whether or not you will provide the associate with any performance bonuses or incentives.

If the term of the associate agreement expires after one year, the associate agreement will need to be rewritten with the new compensation package or contain language permitting it to automatically be renewed with new compensation terms.

Benefits

In addition to the associate's compensation, will you provide any employee benefits such as health insurance, disability insurance, paid personal leave for vacations, paid professional leave for attending continuing education and other business functions? Will you pay for the associate's malpractice insurance, pay for the associate's continuing education, dues and other business expenses? The number of benefits offered in the marketplace varies considerably from practice to practice. Usually those associate agreements that are part of an eventual buy-in will provide more benefits than just a straight associate relationship.

ASSOCIATE AGREEMENTS

Pros: • Agreement must be in writing whether an employee or independent
          contractor
        • Agreement must be in writing to avoid misunderstandings
        • Agreement must avoid ambiguities within the terms of the agreement

Cons: • A written agreement increases the complexity of the transaction

---

The Associate Should Be an Employee

The associate should be hired as your employee and not an independent contractor. Many veterinarians desire to treat their associates as independent contractors to avoid withholding employment taxes and unemployment taxes from the amounts paid to the associate. However, whether the associate is an employee or independent contractor is often based on a number of common law factors that may or may not be present in the relationship. These factors vary from state to state depending upon specific rulings by the appellate courts of each state. More importantly, the Internal Revenue Service has developed a list of 20 factors that it examines in making a determination whether a worker is an employee or an independent contractor for tax purposes. In normal associate veterinary relationships, the vast majority of associates would be classified as employees. If you treat your associate as an independent contractor, you could be subjecting yourself and your practice to an IRS audit and potential penalties and interest charges.

Many veterinarians are unwilling to classify their associates as employees because of the problems that can develop if their associate does not work out and they are forced to terminate the relationship. The hiring veterinarian is frequently uncomfortable about claims for unemployment filed by the terminated associate. Veterinarians need to accept the fact that unemployment insurance fees are simply a cost of doing business. They also need to have their lawyers examine their individual state laws to determine whether they are protected from payment on unemployment claims if they terminate the employee during an "orientation" or "probationary period" established to determine if the employee will work out with the practice. Assuming that your state law permits "trial periods" for purposes of unemployment benefits, you could terminate the relationship within the trial period without being exposed to additional fees for unemployment claims by the terminated employee.

Veterinarians also need to know that they will not be able to avoid discrimination claims by having their associates classified as independent contractors versus employees. Most state and federal discrimination laws are not based on the worker being classified as an employee versus an independent contractor.

Covenant Not to Compete is Frequently Enforceable Only if an Associate Veterinarian is an Employee

Probably the most compelling reason to treat your associate as an employee is that under certain states' laws, a covenant not to compete is enforceable only against an employee and not against an independent contractor.

A covenant not to compete is a contractual term whereby the associate veterinarian agrees not to operate a competing veterinary practice within a reasonable geographic area surrounding the veterinary practice for a reasonable length of time. Covenants not to compete are very important for veterinary practices because they prohibit an associate veterinarian from leaving the employment of the practice and competing with the client base that he or she has created a relationship with while employed by the practice. This effectively protects the "good will" or value of the veterinary practice.

It is clear that a non-competition contract term is a restraint on the ability of an associate veterinarian to conduct his or her trade. However, the vast majority of states have held that an otherwise fair covenant will not be struck down merely because it is a restraint on the associate veterinarian's ability to earn a living. Thus, the majority of courts around the country prefer to protect the sanctity of the contract to protect the employing veterinarian's practice over striking the contract term as a restraint on trade.

TREATING AN ASSOCIATE AS AN EMPLOYEE

Pros: • Avoids risks of IRS audit if not an independent contractor
• Avoids some states' laws voiding non-competition provisions

Cons: • Is more expensive to an employer

Certain states, such as Colorado, generally prohibit the application of a covenant not to compete against any employee unless the employee falls within the statutory or common law standard. In order for a veterinary practice to have an enforceable non-competition agreement, the associate veterinarian must meet the following definition: "Executive and management personnel and officers and employees who constitute professional staff to executive and management personnel." C.R.S. 8-12-113 (l)(d). A veterinary associate would certainly be considered professional staff within this definition. Therefore, if your associate is an employee, the associate would be subject to a reasonable covenant not to compete if such a covenant is included as part of his or her employment agreement. If your associate is treated as an independent contractor, a non-competition agreement would not be enforceable.

Contract Terms to Protect Your Practice

In addition to the above business issues, most employers are concerned with protecting their practices in the event that the associate relationship is not successful. How, you ask, can you protect your practice from an associate whom you have trained and confided with, often for a period of years, who has treated a significant number of your clients and who has developed a significant relationship with your patients and staff? In addition to treating your associate as an employee and providing a written employment agreement with the above terms, the associate agreement should contain the following clauses:

Ownership of Patient Records

Almost all of the associate agreements we have reviewed or drafted have contained a clause stating that all patient records are owned by the employer veterinarian. While this appears to protect the employer from losing clients to the associate, this protection is illusory. We all know that any client, at any time, has the right to request copies of their pet's veterinary records and to transfer their treatment to another veterinarian. If the associate agreement does not contain an enforceable covenant not to compete prohibiting the associate from practicing within a reasonable area of your practice, this clause will offer little or no protection for you, the hiring veterinarian.

Nonsolicitation Clauses

Under most states' laws, an associate can solicit the clients that he or she treated or became acquainted with while employed unless bound by an associate agreement that prohibits him or her from soliciting. This is equally true for an associate who solicits coworkers and other employees of the hiring veterinarian. Accordingly, it is extremely important that the associate agreement contain language prohibiting the associate from soliciting clients and coworkers. Contrary to popular belief, there is no common law protection from this type of solicitation for the hiring veterinarian after the associate leaves his or her employment. There is however a remedy for a hiring veterinarian who learns that an associate is or was soliciting the clients of the practice while still employed by the hiring veterinarian. Further, under most states' laws it is a breach of the employee's duty of loyalty to solicit clients of the hiring veterinarian's practice prior to leaving his or her employment, and there is a specific remedy available for the hiring veterinarian as we will discuss under the Remedies section of this chapter.

Trade Secret Protection

Any associate working for your practice has access to certain business information that you want to protect. If your associate becomes a former associate, you will want the right to prevent the associate from utilizing this business information. The business information may be protected under most states' laws if it can be classified and maintained as a trade secret. Associate agreements need to contain broad language prohibiting the associate from utilization of the hiring veterinarian's trade secrets. However, in much the same fashion as the contract term providing the hiring veterinarian with ownership interest in the patient records, this protection is also illusory. In order for a hiring veterinarian to protect his or her trade secrets, the records and information must meet the definition of a "trade secret" under the specific state's law, and specific steps must be followed to protect the trade secret. If the business information is not a "trade secret" under the applicable state laws or if proper steps to protect the business information have not been taken, then the ability to protect the business information is lost. Courts around the country focus on a variety of factors to consider whether or not a trade secret exists. Some of the more common factors are:

- How widely the information is known outside of the particular practice
- How widely the information is known by employees and others involved in the practice
- The steps taken to guard the secrecy of the information
- The value of the information
- The cost or effort involved in the development of the information
- The cost and effort that would be required to duplicate or be acquired by a third party

In practice, a trade secret can be any information that provides a business with a competitive edge in the marketplace. Some common examples of business information that may constitute a trade secret in a veterinary office include client lists, patient charts, and marketing strategies.

CONTRACT TERMS

Pros:
- Must contain nonsolicitation provisions to prevent solicitation by associate who is not violating noncompetition provisions
- Should prohibit use of hiring veterinarian's trade secrets, including client list

Cons:
- Nonsolicitation clause must be used with noncompete provisions to be effective
- Hiring veterinarians must take steps to protect the secrecy of the information that they want classified as a trade secret

---

Covenants Not to Compete

A covenant not to compete prohibits a terminated associate from operating a competing practice within a geographic area for a set period of time. This is distinguished from Nonsolicitation provisions that prohibit an associate from soliciting specific existing clients or coworkers regardless of where the former associate is practicing. Under most state's laws, covenants not to compete are enforceable only if they are reasonable in the geographic location that the associate is prohibited from practicing within and reasonable in length of time. The covenant not to compete cannot be too broad in defining the area within which the associate is prohibited from competing. Courts commonly will consider the area around the practice that clients are drawn from in determining whether or not the geographic area is reasonable. The reasonableness of the length of time of the covenant not to compete is also of concern for most courts. Certain states will not allow the length of time to be excessive. Ultimately, the question of "What are reasonable geographic and time restrictions?" will depend on the location of the practice and the facts relative to each transaction.

It is important to keep in mind that most courts measure the geographic area limitation radius as a bird flies as opposed to the distance it takes to drive the roads to a particular competing location. This rule is very relevant when an employing veterinarian attempts to enforce a covenant not to compete against a former employee who has set up a practice in a location close to the outside distance of the non-competition agreement. In this scenario, one or both of the veterinarians may measure the distance by driving between the former employer's location and the employee's new location.

It is additionally important to understand that if a court determines that the covenant not to compete is unreasonable in geographic location or length of time, the court may void the entire agreement or the specific covenant not to compete, or may judicially modify the length of time or geographic location of the covenant to make it reasonable. Courts around the country differ on their preferences when faced with this issue. If the employing veterinarian is located in a state that prefers to judicially modify the terms of the non-competition agreement, the employing veterinarian should take an aggressive position on what is reasonable. The employing veterinarian can always choose to settle with a former employee if he or she chooses not to attempt to take the issue before a court. However, it is a good possibility that a former associate veterinarian will choose not to violate an aggressive covenant not to compete in order to avoid the costs of litigation.

Attorneys Fees

It is important that your associate agreement contain language permitting you to recover your attorneys' fees if you are forced to file a lawsuit to prevent a terminated associate from violating a covenant not to compete. Most states require an attorneys' fees provision in an associate agreement before the enforcing veterinarian is entitled to recover the sums that he or she has paid to his or her attorneys. Further, having such language in your associate agreement may influence a former associate to comply with its terms since the associate would have to pay your attorneys' fees as well as his or her own.

Liquidated Damage Provision

The majority of states permit parties to negotiate into contracts the amount of damages that a party will be entitled to recover if a breach of the contract or covenant occurs. These contract terms are called "liquidated damage provisions" and can be an effective tool to prevent an associate from violating a covenant not to compete or a Nonsolicitation provision of an associate agreement.

Associate Agreement Must Be Assignable by Employer

The associate agreement must provide that the employing veterinarian is entitled to assign the agreement to a new purchaser or a new entity. This would be very important to the employing veterinarian if he or she would decide or need to sell or restructure the business. The value of a veterinary practice is dependent upon preventing key employee veterinarians from competing with the business after the acquisitions.

Both the Employing Veterinarian and the Employee Veterinarian Must Give "Consideration" When Employee Veterinarian Enters into a Covenant Not to Compete

All states require that both parties to a contract give "consideration" in order for the contract to be enforceable. The legal concept of consideration requires that each party either give some right, interest, or benefit or give up a forbearance or detriment. This is also true for associate agreements and covenants not to compete. In order for the associate agreement and the covenant not to compete to be enforceable, the employing veterinarian and the associate veterinarian must have each given consideration. An associate veterinarian obviously meets the legal obligation by agreeing to the restrictive covenant not to compete. The same can be said for the employing veterinarian if the associate veterinarian enters into the associate agreement prior to becoming an employee.

A problem develops when the employing veterinarian imposes the associate agreement upon the associate veterinarian after he or she has worked for the employing veterinarian. The employing veterinarian has arguably not given any consideration if the associate veterinarian has already been an employee. If a court rules that consideration has not been given as a result of prior employment, the contract containing the covenant not to compete cannot be enforced, and the employing veterinarian is at risk of the associate taking a portion of the clients of the practice.

In certain states, it has been held that the employing veterinarian has given consideration by permitting the associate veterinarian to retain his or her job. However, courts in many states have ruled that the employing veterinarian has not met his or her obligation simply by permitting the associate veterinarian to retain his or her job. In light of the uncertainty of this issue around the country, it is advisable that the employing veterinarian provides the existing associate veterinarian with a sum of money for his or her entering into the associate agreement. This is especially important for an employing veterinarian in the event he or she wants to sell the veterinary practice. In this case, the buyer will reduce his or her offer for the practice based upon a perception of the risk that an associate veterinarian would leave and legally compete with the practice. An employing veterinarian can choose to give an existing associate veterinarian a benefit other than a cash payment. There is no specific requirement on what the benefit needs to be or the value of the benefit. One example of consideration other than cash is payment of professional liability insurance, if not already provided, or additional funds for continuing education.

COVENANT NOT TO COMPETE

Pros:
- If enforceable, will protect the hiring veterinarian's client base
- Contains attorneys' fees provision that will influence an associate veterinarian's decision if the associate considers violating the contract
- Contains liquidated damage provisions that will influence an associate veterinarian's decision if the associate considers violating the contract

Cons:
- Requires hiring veterinarian to meet state law requirements to have an enforceable covenant not to compete
- Requires that both hiring and employee veterinarians meet state law requirement of consideration to have enforceable agreement containing covenant not to compete

---

Tips to Conducting Negotiations with Your Associate

How can the terms of an associate agreement be negotiated without damaging the relationship of the hiring veterinarian and the associate veterinarian? The inherent problem in these negotiations is that there are conflicting goals. The goal of the hiring veterinarian is to obtain contract terms to protect his or her practice in the event that the relationship is not successful. This is in sharp contrast to the goal of the associate veterinarian, who is interested in contract terms that will permit him or her flexibility if the relationship fails. There is a point in any negotiation of an associate agreement when these equally compelling goals conflict and hard feelings can develop. Frequently, these hard feelings have long-term effects upon the relationship of the parties to the negotiations.

There are a number of steps that a hiring veterinarian can take to minimize the risk of hard feelings developing during the negotiations.

Negotiate in a Neutral Site

The hiring veterinarian can conduct the negotiations in a neutral site where there is no perceived power position. This approach is intended to place the associate veterinarian at ease. If a hiring veterinarian conducts the negotiations in his or her office, he or she is more likely to be perceived by the associate veterinarian as being in the power position.

Describe Expectations

The hiring veterinarian can describe his or her expectations of the associate veterinarian and his or her goals at the beginning of the negotiations. If the intention of the hiring veterinarian is to have a Nonsolicitation provision and covenant not to compete, he should bring up this issue at an early point in the negotiations and explain why he or she feels strongly about having these provisions. A common explanation for a hiring veterinarian to offer is that the associate agreements are designed to protect the hiring veterinarian until the two veterinarians have decided that the associate should stay with the practice and become an owner. The hiring veterinarian should communicate that should the hiring veterinarian and the associate veterinarian decide to stay together, the associate agreement will be restructured at that time to be more beneficial for the associate veterinarian.

It is also important that the hiring veterinarian talk to the associate veterinarian early in the negotiations about what the associate's expectations for compensation will be. There is no benefit to delaying communication on this issue.

Do Not Rush the Associate

It is also important that the hiring veterinarian give the associate veterinarian enough time to analyze and fully understand what is being proposed. The associate needs to have an opportunity to have his or her own attorney review the draft associate agreement. A hiring veterinarian should keep in mind that this may be the first time the associate veterinarian has dealt with associate agreements and that he or she may be very uncomfortable about the entire process.

Your Remedies Against an Associate Who Violates the Associate Agreement and Covenants

Despite your considerable thought and consideration, your associate has not met your expectations. Instead of having the extra time that you always wanted, you are spending your time dealing with a disgruntled staff and complaints from unhappy clients. You terminate the associate and are shocked to learn a short time later that your now-former associate has set up a practice within the geographic area of your covenant not to compete and is soliciting your clients and employees. What are your remedies against your former associate?

A hiring veterinarian with an enforceable and properly drafted associate agreement has several remedies available. The first remedy is an injunction. An injunction will take care of the immediate need of stopping the former associate from continuing to damage your practice by soliciting your clients and employees and competing with your practice. A properly drafted associate agreement will waive certain legal requirements to make obtaining a temporary injunction more probable until the case can be taken to trial. The second remedy for the hiring veterinarian is the remedy of monetary damages. If the associate agreement contained a liquidated damage provision, you will be entitled to recover the amount that was agreed upon. If the associate agreement did not contain a liquidated damage provision, you will be able to recover the damages that you have incurred based upon the profits that you lost as a result of the actions of your former associate. If you are able to prove that the former associate solicited your clients prior to leaving your employment, you are entitled to recover the compensation that you paid the associate for the period of time that he or she was soliciting clients while in your employ. In addition to the above, if you have included an attorneys' fees provision in the associate agreement, you will be entitled to recover your attorneys' fees if you prevail.

Hiring an associate veterinarian is an important decision that could have serious adverse impacts upon your practice. Since no one can predict with any certainty that the associate relationship will be successful, it is very important that you have a well-drafted associate agreement to protect you and your practice in the event that your associate decides to start his or her own practice at your expense.

NEGOTIATIONS WITH YOUR ASSOCIATE

Pros:
- If in the form of a written agreement, will make parties feel more comfortable
- Prepares parties to consult with legal and tax advisors to determine consequences of associate agreement
- Establish an employee for non-competition provisions
- Clearly establish agreement of parties on:
  ✓ compensation
  ✓ inventions or innovations created during work

Cons:
- May delay doctor beginning to work with practice
- Can be expensive if in the form of a properly drafted associate agreement

---

APPENDIX A

Personal and Practice Value Assessment

PERSONAL/PRACTICE VALUE ASSESSMENT (short form)

WHAT YOU OWN	200__		200__	
	% Total		% Total	
	Amount	Assets	Amount	Assets
Accounts Receivable	$	%	$	%
Real Estate (w/o practice)	$	%	$	%
Personal Money Market Funds	$	%	$	%
Retirement Plan Share (w/ IRAs)	$	%	$	%
Other Income Investments	$	%	$	%
Annual Practice Gross	$	%	$	%
Market Value of Home	$	%	$	%
Life Insurance Cash Value	$	%	$	%
Personal Property Value	$	%	$	%
Other Assets of Value	$	%	$	%
TOTAL ASSETS	$	100%	$	100%

WHAT YOU OWE	% Total		% Total	
	Amount	Liability	Amount	Liability
Balance on Practice Debt	$	%	$	%
Balance on Mortgage	$	%	$	%
Balance on Long Term Loans	$	%	$	%
Accounts Payable	$	%	$	%
Bills & Short Term Notes	$	%	$	%
Taxes Payable	$	%	$	%
Other Obligations Due	$	%	$	%
TOTAL LIABILITIES	$	100%	$	100%

NET WORTH COMPUTATIONS (from short form)

_____ – _____ = $ _____
   (assets)   (liabilities)   (net worth)

Compute Your Growth Rate:

1. Net Worth in 200__ (second column)   _____

2. Net Worth in 200__ (first column)   –   _____

3. Increase in 200__ (line 1 minus line 2)   =   _____

4. Growth Rate
   (line 3 x 100, divided by line 2)   _____._____%

5. New Funds Added in 200__ (second column):

   Retirement plan   _____

   Net additions to other savings   _____

   Principal payments on mortgages/loans   _____

   Premiums on cash value life insurance   _____

   Resale of new personal property   _____

6. Total New Funds in 200__ (second column)   _____

7. Return on 200__ Assets (line 3 minus line 6) $_____

8. True Rate of Return:
   (Multiply line 7 by 100; divide by line 2)   _____._____%

The Practice Value Elements

Tangible Assets are convertible to cash on the open market. This includes yard sale, auction, or private advertisement. These items have an intrinsic value that can be determined by people who use, trade, or study these items.

Client Records can produce income if properly maintained and nurtured. In a competitive economy, their value is tied to the likelihood of converting these assets to the buyer's use. There is an element of risk in this process, however. Failure to treat your clients with respect and care will have a negative effect on the value of your records. Determining the value of client records requires an intimate understanding of the practice and the function and operations of veterinary practice.

Net Excess Earnings express the ability of the practice to be a viable business entity. Profitability is the measure of the spread between expenses and productivity. Net excess earnings is recovered over years and therefore carries a fiscal risk.

These three elements express the sum of the values that represent the monetary value of the practice. This value is determined for the day the data is complete and calculated. The three elements are added together. Any one of the three can change at any time, and with it, the value of the practice.

Tangible Assets

Tangible assets are simple and can be determined easily. These are:

- *Real Estate*

  Land and buildings that directly support the practice. In some practices, real estate is held in a separate entity that receives rent. Should it not be offered for sale with the practice, it has no asset value to the practice. However, a long-term lease is needed, and all leasehold improvements have a value.

- *Equipment*
These are the tools and instruments of the practice. Equipment can be valued by an appraiser whose judgement is trusted and is generally worth 60 percent of replacement value. Some items of equipment are so old, however, that they have no intrinsic value.

- *Inventory*
Current cost of items that get used up. The size of inventory should not exceed a six-month supply. Well-managed practices will operate with a two- to three-week supply of many items. Excessive inventory is frequently found along with other management problems, which reduces the value of the practice.

- *Investments*
Anything that is owned by the practice and is not directly related to the performance of veterinary medicine (loosely defined). This could be cash reserves held in long-term certificates of deposit.

- *Liabilities*
Any debt outstanding to the practice for any reason whatsoever. The current payments (this year's payment amounts) are an expense. Liabilities are the value of the principal remaining beyond the current year. Also included here is accounts payable.

- *Working Capital*
Greenbacks in the refrigerator, deposits in the bank accounts, accounts receivable.

The sum of all the above items is the value of Tangible Assets.

Client Records

At Veterinary Practice Consultants®, we use "Client Classes" during our medical record audit. The client classes, or categories, are based on the number of times the clients came in during the previous year. We know we are conservative, since the studies (AVMA and Pfizer) show that good clients come into preferred animal practices three to six times a year.

- Class I includes clients who came in more than once in the past 12 months.
- Class II includes clients who came in once in the past 12 months.
- Class III includes clients who came in less than once in the past 12 months.

From our experience in companion animal veterinary practices for over two decades, we have determined a very conservative multiplier value for each class: Class I is 1.5 to 2.0; Class II is 1.0; and Class III is 0.5. Certainly, some individuals in each class will be worth more than the multiplier value, and a few will be worth less. There are also individual clients who have more than one pet. Do not dwell on such ideas. Think of statistics.

✓ **Client class values** are determined by counting the number of clients and how many times they come into the practice. It is often easier to ask a banker for a risk factor than to ask your veterinary software to tell you about your clients, but tell they must! This should be part of the standard information you are receiving from the data you pour into your computer.

✓ Each practice has different criteria for the determination of an **"active client."** One of the factors is a time frame cut-off. During this time, a certain number of clients "drift" away (a practice with an aggressive recall system with every third reminder will usually have close to 100 percent active clients). This defines the retention rate. If you started the period with 1000 clients and finish with 880, you have a retention rate of 88 percent.

The **Average Client Transaction [ACT]** is defined simply: How many times did the cash register go "KA-CHING!"? In other words, how much money came in? Divide dollars by transactions.

The **Present Value of Future Earnings** is a concept your banker and your bookie understand with precision. Consider this: If I offer to give you one dollar next year at this time, you may very well be willing to loan me 96 cents today based on the expected loss of buying power of the dollar over a year. Or you may only offer me 96 cents for six months if you don't have a lot of confidence in my ability to stay alive on the mean streets. Inversely, if you give me that dollar right now, you will want more than a dollar return in one year. This is the concept of Present Value of Future Earnings and is related to both trust and risk, as well as to the stability of the practice (client return rate).

Risk is appraised in economic terms by the quality of the economic community and its robust vigor, as well as in the business plan or history of your business. Most small businesses in a good niche in a healthy economy attract a risk of 5 or a discount of 20 percent. A stable, competitive veterinary practice, positioned for a seamless transition, attracts a rate of 4. This is a discount of 25 percent. In veterinary practice, there are more variables, as discussed in Chapter 2. Ask your banker where your community viability stands.

Calculation of value of client records is done in two steps:

1. **ACT**   *times*
   Retention   *times*
   Risk   *equals*
                  'ACT' (adjusted average client transaction)

2. **Class count**   *times*
   Multiplier   *times*
   'ACT'   *equals*
                  Class Value

The sum of the three classes is the value of the Client Records.

Net Excess Earnings

Most accountants and many business people have gotten past expense control as the dominant objective and have moved on to income enhancement. However, it is not the gross but the difference between gross and expense that is the measure of the business.

The **Net Excess Earnings** is the money left over after all legitimate expenses have been paid. This includes the clinical and managerial duties salary for the owner(s), reasonable rent to owner if real estate is held by the owner of the practice, interest payment on loans, and ROI (about 6-7 percent of gross income). It also includes all balance sheet expenses that are not regularly included on the profit and loss statement. The issue of return on investment [ROI] must be addressed carefully. Any payments to the owner that are not defined as salary may well be a return on investment and must be identified.

In the event there is no actual net excess earnings, the value of the practice approaches the value of the tangible assets.

It is the *projection* of the net excess earnings that will be the third measure of the practice. Growth and risk are the operations.

Growth for the last three years is annualized (percentage growth over the last three years is divided by three). A growth of less than 8 percent pretty much defines a stagnant practice. Growth will be projected for three years into the future and the present value of those future earnings is the value sought. The formula for this calculations is

Current Net   *times*
Growth (%)   *times*
Risk Discount   *equals*
                         Present Value of Future Earnings

Why is a particular number of years used when projecting earnings and future growth? We have found that three years is the length of time during which the full repercussions of managerial decisions are effective. This means managerial, medical, and personnel decisions made three years previously are no longer of primary significance. This also means that an owner cannot sell more than three years' worth of future earnings because after that length of time, the earnings are the result of things that happened after the sale.

WORKSHEET FOR AN AVERAGE PRACTICE VALUATION

Tangible Assets
- Real Estate   _____ *Determined by appraisal*
- Equipment   _____ *Replacement value times 0.6*
- Inventory   _____ *Cost*
- Working Capital
  - Accounts Receivable   _____
  - Cash   _____
  - Liquid Assets   _____ *Stocks/bonds cash value*
- Liabilities
  - Loans   _____ *Principal cost beyond this year*
  - Accounts Payable   _____

Sum of Tangible Assets _____

Client Records
ACT $_____
Retention 84   *An average practice will have an 84% retention.*
Risk   0.75 *A stable, transferable practice in a healthy economy with appropriate growth can attract a discount rate of 25%.*

- Class I   ____ × 1.5 × 'ACT' = $_____
- Class II   ____ × 1.0 × 'ACT' = $_____
- Class III   ____ × 0.5 × 'ACT' = $_____

Sum of Client Records _____

Net Excess Earnings (example)
For a Net Excess Earnings of $17,000 in the most recent year; an annual gross growth of 13% for last three years; a risk of four with a discount rate of 25%.

First year $17,000 × 1.13 = $19,210 × .800 = $15,370
Second year $19,210 × 1.13 = $21,710 × .640 = $13,890
Third year $21,710 × 1.13 = $24,530 × .512 = $12,560

Sum of Present Value of Future Earnings $41,820

Sum of Tangible Assets   _____
Sum of Client Records   _____
Sum of Present Value   _____

Value of Practice _____

Notes

APPENDIX B

Compensation

EXAMPLE #1

The objective is to determine the veterinarian's equitable compensation and personal eligibility for supplemental performance compensation, and their respective weighted percentages. It shall be computed as follows:

A. Base pay shall be 20 percent of the previous year's personal production, divided into 24 pay periods, payable on the 15th and last day of each month of the year.

B. Productivity (incentive) compensation shall increase 0.5 percent each year that the personal contribution to practice programs increases (maximum of 22.5 percent). Payment will be made monthly by the following formula:

1. Improvement of patient-client service survey results to reflect that 75 percent or greater of the respondents rate the veterinarian's services as "excellent."
(Assigned Percentage: 20 percent)
2. Individual's active involvement in community activity that promotes community image, health, and/or wellness as well as the veterinarian's identity to community members.
(Assigned Percentage: 10 percent)
3. Veterinarian's timely and satisfactory performance of all administrative and non-patient care responsibilities that may be assigned from time to time by the practice leadership.
(Assigned Percentage: 10 percent)
4. Evaluation by the paraprofessional team of harmony, synergy, and quality of practice performance as part of practice team.
(Assigned Percentage: 10 percent)
5. Attainment or surpassment of practice's financial projections for the fiscal year.
(Assigned Percentage: 50 percent)

NOTE: *The above objectives are merely examples; actual objectives should be jointly developed by the associate veterinarian and practice ownership.*

Initialed this date _____, 20__ Practice Ownership ___ Veterinarian ___

STANDARDS FOR SUPPLEMENTAL COMPENSATION

Appraisal category	Category weight	Total points possible	Actual points
I. Quality of Care of Services	25%	25	_____
II. Productivity	25%	25	_____
III. Staff Relationships	20%	20	_____
IV. Financial Factors	20%	20	_____
V. Community Role	10%	10	_____
TOTALS	100%	100	_____

Range of Points	Compensation
93–100	$_____
85–92	$_____
77–84	$_____
67–76	$_____
<66	$_____

EXAMPLE #3

Putting Balance Back into the Equation

*Sabbatical—the year the land and vineyards are to re-
main fallow and the debtors are to be released.*
—Webster's Dictionary

After almost two decades of operating and visiting veterinary facilities, I am acutely aware that many veterinarians do not lead balanced
lives (myself included). The pressures in our industry from government
regulations, associates, staff, and clients put our practice owners into
health-threatening situations. The new associate is usually seen as a
great labor-saving device, not as great as a caring spouse, but almost.
We need to take a few months to train new associates to the practice's
ways, and in some cases, those "few months" can reach almost a year
before a productivity return is seen.

Alternatives

Veterinarians need a release, and snatching a quick set of tennis or
nine holes of golf, while efficacious and worthy of pursuit, does not
provide a sufficient break to refresh and reinvigorate. In many communities, you can spot the veterinarian who vigorously pursues excellence in a manner similar to the practice, doing the right things for the
wrong reasons, playing an appropriate game, or really trying to get
better at a skill. In reality, many "golfers" are closing a deal, making a
contact, or softening someone up for a later favor. This does not lead
to balance. The "recurring and sacred" three-day weekend comes
closer to this recharge goal, since the first day is for "unwind," the center day is for "play," and the last day for that dreaded "gear-up" to get
back into the grind.

The Sabbatical

In addition to deferred compensation plans and creative annual benefits, we increasingly see sabbatical agreements as part of a multi-vet-
erinarian practice's work plan. The sabbatical should be considered because it offers multiple benefits for the individual and organization.
The sabbatical provides an extended period of time for the veterinar-

ian to recharge and recommit, to discover new experiences and new knowledge, to identify and explore interests beyond the practice environment that can be with him or her now and after the job is over. Unfortunately, far too many veterinarians still go into retirement (willingly or unwillingly) having nothing to do but travel and spend money.

In return for a 12- to 24-week sabbatical (some are actually 6 to 12 months), the practice gets a revitalized veterinarian as well as a chance to see how the other professionals on the team can perform out of the shadow of the sabbatical veterinarian. Often, the sabbatical can be a source of many exciting ideas. It is not unrealistic for a practice owner to take a sabbatical at a human hospital, marketing agency, or larger community service business, watching the administrative operations and strategic marketing plans evolve. Some have taken an Outward Bound-type experience, learning about themselves, their inner strengths, and developing leadership skills while exploring new outdoor activity skills. Some have even taken their families overseas, practiced veterinary medicine in a foreign country, and returned far more thankful than knowledgeable. The veterinarian can usually bring back ideas and concepts from other healthcare facilities that will benefit the practice, the staff, and the clients who seek veterinary expertise.

When most veterinarians think sabbatical, they think of returning to a veterinary school to learn additional practice skills. Continuing education in a new specialty field is not the diversity that should be pursued to prevent professional burnout, but it should be an alternative if the signs of practice burnout have already emerged. Some veterinarians will want to enter the academic environment in the fields of management or marketing, for a three-week or three-month course of study, such as the highly structured programs at Harvard, the Wharton School of Business at the University of Pennsylvania, or the professor exchange program of Tufts Veterinary Teaching Hospital.

If 12 weeks is not possible, you can make a two-week adventure occur, possibly a cruise, a dude ranch adventure, or something else you have NEVER done with your significant other. Yes, take that special other person and share an experience that makes you forget the practice, the bills, and the other challenges at home. The guidelines for sabbaticals can be easily established, such as for every five years a veterinarian spends full-time with the practice, one sabbatical will be funded. These are budgeted by the practice at one per year, with the most tenured veterinarian getting the first year's opportunity, the second most tenured getting the second year's, and so on. The subsidy for the sabbatical will equal the average monthly salary of the veterinarian for the previous two years plus an extra $5000 up-front activity stipend to be used specifically for the new adventure or activity (this may even pay for a wardrobe expansion if required by the sabbatical environment). If it is budgeted, it will occur in a well-managed practice—honest!

Follow that Dream

If Mama ain't happy, ain't nobody happy
—Blues song

Sabbaticals may not be desirable or possible for everyone, but each of us can still "follow that dream." Fulfilling dreams brings balance. Concentrated attention, more than just time, is usually the essential ingredient required to fulfill a dream. The hardest thing for any practice owner to do well is to relax, to let go, to recreate a new person through recreation. We want to and we certainly need to, but our stress just will not allow us to do it.

In some practices, having the new associate carry an olive branch to every practice in the city starts a new adventure for all the practices (give the associate the time and make him/her do it). Egos often don't let the established doctors break the paradigm, but then again, everyone was a new graduate once and understands the trepidation of approaching the old codgers of the profession. Such a gesture increases the number of opportunities for improved interchanges. Breaking the paradigm STARTS with accepting the obvious fact that habits do exist, and those that exist only because "we've always done it this way" are the ones that should be adjusted first. When a new associate can influence a habit of unknown origin (paradigm), he or she will feel more involved in practice success.

So if you are one of those stressed veterinarians who cannot afford to take a sabbatical, forget the excuses and find a cause that you can believe in enough to force yourself to make the time for it. The Christian Veterinarians travel to third world countries (and New Mexico), the Chamber of Commerce has exchange programs, even the Boy Scouts have summer camping programs that need skilled veterinarians. If you cannot find a reason to invest in youth or in the developing third world, there are always the environment and the agricultural needs of Native Americans. There are also planned activities by conservation groups to count whales, inventory islands, or help return part of this planet to Mother Nature for the good of us all.

Naturally, little in our veterinary degree programs prepared us for these moments of truth in our own lives. Family counseling is not a critical national board item. As human beings, we require the balance that work and play provide. Without that balance, we are less able to take a visionary stance and less able to manage our own people with a true human perspective. If all we ever show our staffs are our working sides, we are likely to lead them into imbalance as well.

Having established the thesis of "get a life," consider the family you have. If you think having to repair a practice damaged by neglect and lack of maintenance is difficult, you ain't seen nothing compared to a broken family. Should that concept seem radical to you, you need help. Now.

Seek Adventures

As a child, most of us had dreams that were put aside. A "practice break" allows those dreams to reemerge. As in the movie "City Slickers," it's still possible to go on a cattle drive. In Tennessee, there is a school for learning how to drive draft horses. In Colorado, we have white water rafting scenery like you have never seen! The time requirement for this can be as short as one week. Physical labor has its own rewards: to prove that youth is still in us and that we can still learn a new skill.

Some have taken a two-week motorcycle tour on rugged back country roads (as in Baja, California). Others have pursued a lifelong interest in the sea and learned to sail, first in smaller then larger boats. Another adventure took several vacations, after the initial "practice break," considering that the Caribbean Sea had to be explored by scuba diving. In another case, the "practice break" adventure led to becoming an equine dressage trainer. There are a few who have taken to the mountains, some free climbing, some hiking, some with extensive rope work, looking for the next higher mountain or the view that will make the memories that last forever. Some people pursue an interest that keeps on giving, like using their practice-break adventure to become a soccer or football official and spending every weekend on the gridiron.

Finding the Time

Most veterinarians will claim they are too busy, but that is only an excuse. If they get admitted to the cardiac care unit, the practice continues. When they want to go to a conference, the practice continues. When there is an accident or family emergency that takes the veterinarian out of the flow, the practice continues. We all have the same 24 hours to work with in each day; some of us are more productive, more effective, or more flexible than others.

Time management courses abound. None of them has ever stretched the hour past 60 minutes or the day past 24 hours. Time management starts with the assessment(s) of practice paradigms, and many staff members do this daily. No one listens, but they do it anyway. The true leader has the humility to acknowledge that everyone needs to break unsuccessful old habits and learn successful new ones. This individual is rare. The process and the need for self-assessment of paradigms is true in practice management as well as in personal life.

The enthusiastic reception the sabbatical concept typically receives in healthcare settings indicates that it should be used more, not less, in veterinary practices. The sabbatical is still uncommon, although we are beginning to see it more often than a few years ago. Have you given thought to what you might accomplish with a large gift of unscheduled time? Do you have a dream that could be fulfilled, if you took the time and effort to make it come true? Give your dreams a chance. They will serve you well.

APPENDIX C

Employment
Agreement

EMPLOYMENT AGREEMENT

THIS CONTRACT is made and entered into this _____ day of _____, 20__, by and between _____, D.V.M. hereinafter called "Employer,", and _____, D.V.M. hereinafter called "Employee."

1. Employee is duly licensed to practice veterinary medicine in the state of Colorado and desires to accept employment to practice veterinary medicine as an employee of Employer.

2. Employer is engaged in the practice of veterinary medicine in _____, Colorado, as a sole proprietorship and desires to employ Employee in such veterinary practice.

3. Employer has offered Employee employment for such compensation and other benefits under the terms and conditions hereinafter set forth, and Employee is willing to accept employment on such terms. The parties desire to set forth all rights, duties, obligations, and terms of their agreement concerning such employment in writing as hereinafter set forth.

NOW, THEREFORE, in consideration of the mutual covenants, conditions, and terms contained herein, the receipt and sufficiency of which is acknowledged, the parties agree as follows:

1. EMPLOYMENT AND DUTIES

a. SCOPE OF DUTIES: Employer hereby employs Employee, and Employee accepts such employment to render veterinary services. Employee agrees to devote his entire and exclusive working attention to the practice of his profession for Employer and to the performance of such administrative and management duties as required by and of him. The power to supervise the duties to be performed, the manner of performing such duties, and the terms for performance thereof shall be exercised by Employer. Employee agrees that he will at all times faithfully, industriously, and to the best of his ability, experience, and talents, perform all of the duties that may be required of and from him pursuant to the express and implicit terms hereof, to the satisfaction of Employer. Employee shall make available to Employer all information of which Employee shall have any knowledge and shall make all suggestions and recommendations that will be of mutual benefit to Employer and himself. Employer shall assign patients and work to Employee and shall designate the days and hours of employment.

b. EXCLUSIVE SERVICE: Beginning _____, the date of this Agreement, Employee works exclusively for Employer. Employee agrees to devote his entire working time and attention to the practice of his profession of veterinary treatment for Employer and to the performance of such other administrative and management activities as may be required by and for Employer. The expenditure of outside business, or charitable, community, or outside professional activities shall not be deemed a breach of this Contract, provided such activities do not interfere with the service required to be rendered to Employer hereunder. Employee shall not, without the express prior written consent of Employer, directly or indirectly render services of a professional nature to or for any person or firm other than Employer for compensation during the term of this contract, nor shall Employee engage in any activity competitive with or adverse to Employer's business or practice, in any capacity whether individually, as a partner, or an officer, director, employee or shareholder of any corporation or limited liability company member, or as a trustee, agent, fiduciary, or other representative of any group, body, organization, or activity without Employer's explicit written consent.

c.   EMPLOYER'S AUTHORITY: Employee agrees to observe and comply with all reasonable rules and regulations duly adopted by Employer either verbally or in writing, respecting the performance of his duties and services. Employee specifically understands that Employer shall have final authority over all professional matters such as the acceptance or refusal of any client or patient for whom professional services may be rendered, the setting of Employee's office hours, and the amount of fee to be charged to all clients. The power to direct, control and supervise the manner of, and time for, Employee performing Employee's duties and services, shall be exercised by Employer.

d. RECORDS: Employee shall keep and maintain at all times accurate and legible and complete case histories, progress reports, and records for all clients and patients Employee sees in accordance with procedures and regulations adopted by Employer. All such client and patient case histories, test results, files, reports, records, and information of any kind are deemed to be at all times the sole property of Employer, subject to other disposition only upon appropriate demand of the patient. Upon termination of this Agreement, Employee shall not be entitled to keep, preserve, or reproduce any such records as to any clients or patients for whom services were performed. Employee shall have reasonable access to records upon notice to Employer, but shall not be entitled to make any copies unless a malpractice or other legal proceeding requiring such information has been commenced against the Employee.

Employer agrees to maintain all originals of all records, and if he fails to do so, Employer will indemnify and defend Employee against all claims from clients whose original records have been sent out of the office or destroyed.

2. TERM

The term of this Agreement shall begin on _____, 20___, and shall continue until _____, 20___, unless terminated as hereinafter provided. The parties may renew this Agreement to extend it as they may determine in writing, signed by both parties. At the time of termination, the parties may negotiate a purchase contract. "Terminated" as used herein, means any method whereby the Employer-Employee relationship ceases to exist.

3. COMPENSATION, BENEFITS, AND PROFESSIONAL LIABILITY INSURANCE

For all services rendered by Employee under this Contract, Employer shall pay Employee _____ percent (___%) of Employee's gross production, whichever is greater. "Full-time employment" is defined as _____ (___) hours per week. "Gross production," for this purpose, shall mean the gross fees that are collected from clients for services which that have been performed and completed by Employee. Employer agrees to allow a reasonable opportunity for Employer's office manager to secure financial arrangements for all proposed treatment prior to commencing treatment.

Employee shall pay for, and carry professional liability insurance insuring Employee for professional errors, omissions, negligence, incompetence, and malfeasance committed by Employee. Employee shall provide Employer with a certificate of purchase showing the type and amount of coverage and period of coverage of professional liability insurance. Employer shall have the opportunity to approve said professional liability insurance and coverage prior to execution of this Contract. Employee shall provide proof of professional liability insurance upon request by Employer.

Employee has the opportunity to participate in any group health and/or disability insurance offered to other employees of the practice. All vacation, leave, and personal time off shall be by mutual agreement by the parties and without pay.

4. NEW CLIENTS

Clients who are new to the practice shall be distributed as follows: any client who asks for a specific veterinarian shall be assigned to that veterinarian or be scheduled to the first available appointment the client will accept. If a new client does not ask for a specific veterinarian, the new client shall be assigned to each veterinarian based on appointment book availability and at Employer's discretion and direction.

5. WORKING FACILITIES

Employer shall furnish employee with support services, supplies, equipment, appropriate staffing, and such other facilities and services as may be suitable to his position and adequate for the performance of his duties.

6. FEES

All fees and compensation received or realized as a result of the rendering of professional services by Employee shall belong to and be paid and delivered to Employer. Employer shall have the sole right to determine the amount of fees being charged for Employee's services to patients.

7. INVOLUNTARY TERMINATION

This Contract shall be deemed to be terminated, and the employment relationship between Employee and Employer shall be deemed severed, upon the occurrence of any of the following:

a. Upon the death or disability, during employment of Employee. Disability is defined as permanent disability or temporary disability that prevents Employee from working for a period of sixty (60) consecutive calendar days or more.

b. The suspension, revocation, or cancellation of Employee's right to practice his profession in the State of Colorado.

c. The imposition of any restrictions or limitations by any governmental authority having jurisdiction over Employee to such an extent that he cannot engage in the professional practice for which he was employed.

d. Employee fails or refuses to faithfully and diligently perform the usual and customary duties of his employment or adhere to the provisions of this Contract.

e. Employee fails or refuses to comply with the reasonable policies, standards, and regulations of Employer, which from time to time may be established.

f. Employee conducts himself in an unprofessional, unethical, immoral, or fraudulent manner, or is found guilty of unprofessional or unethical conduct by any board, institution, organization, or professional society having any privilege or right to pass upon the conduct of Employee, or Employee's conduct discredits Employer or is detrimental to the reputation, character, or standing of Employer or violates any of the provisions of the principles of ethics and code of professional conduct.

8. VOLUNTARY TERMINATION

In any event, this Contract may be earlier terminated without cause, by either party hereto upon thirty (30) days written notice. In any case of termination, Employee shall be solely responsible to complete those veterinary procedures for patients whose failure to do so could jeopardize the veterinary health of the patient in the sole opinion of Employer.

9. TESTING

Employee warrants, to the best of his knowledge, that as of the date of this contract, he has not tested positive for HIV or the Hepatitis B Virus.

10. ARBITRATION

Employer and Employee agree that any and all differences, controversies, or claims arising out of or relating to this agreement, or the breach of this agreement and any related documents, shall be submitted to and settled by arbitration in _____, Colorado in accordance with the Commercial Arbitration Rules of the American Arbitration Association. In the event the parties are unable to mutually agree as to the selection of an arbitrator, each party shall select an arbitrator, and the two arbitrators shall select a third arbitrator, who shall arbitrate the dispute. Any arbitration shall be final, and absolute. Judgment upon the award may be entered in any court having jurisdiction. The prevailing part shall be entitled to all reasonable costs and expenses including reasonable legal and according fees.

11. RELATIONSHIP BETWEEN THE PARTIES

The parties recognize that the relationship between Employer and Employee shall be that of an Employer-Employee. Notwithstanding anything herein contained to the contrary, Employee shall have the right to make any contracts or commitments for or on behalf of Employer without first obtaining the written consent of Employer.

12. CONSTRUCTION

This Contract shall be governed by the laws of the state of Colorado. The waiver by any party hereto or a breach of any provision of this Contract shall not operate or be construed as a waiver of any subsequent breach by any party. This instrument contains the entire agreement of the parties concerning employment, and may not be changed except by written agreement duly executed by the parties hereto. This Contract shall inure to the benefit of and be binding upon the parties, their successors, heirs, and personal representatives. This Contract shall not be assignable by either party without the written consent of the other party.

13. NOTICES

All notices required or permitted under this Contract shall be in writing and shall be deemed delivered in the United States Mail, postage paid, by certified mail, return receipt requested, addressed as follows:

Employer:

_____, D.V.M.

_____

_____

Employee:

_____, D.V.M.

_____

_____

Such addresses may be changed from time to time by either party by providing written notice in the manner set forth above.

14. ENTIRE AGREEMENT

This Contract contains the entire agreement of the parties, and there are no other promises or conditions in any other agreement whether oral or written. This Contract supersedes any prior written or oral contract between the parties.

15. AMENDMENT

This Contract may be modified or amended, if the amendment is made in writing and signed by both parties.

16. SEVERABILITY

If any provision of this Contract shall be held to be invalid or unenforceable for any reason, the remaining provision shall continue to be valid and enforceable. If a court finds that any provision of this Contract is invalid or unenforceable, but that by limiting such provision it would become valid and enforceable, then such provision shall be deemed to be written, construed, and enforced as so limited.

DATED TO this ____ day of _____, 20__

EMPLOYER:

_____

Date:_____

EMPLOYEE:

_____

Date:_____

APPENDIX D

Bill of Sale

BILL OF SALE

Vet for Sale, P.C. (hereinafter "Seller"), for good and valuable consideration paid by John P. Vet (hereinafter "Purchaser"), the receipt and adequacy of which is acknowledged, does bargain, sell, assign, transfer, and deliver to Purchaser the property listed in the attached Exhibit "1.01" in connection with Seller's Veterinary Practice located at 2222 Vet Way, Denver, Colorado 80204.

Seller warrants and represents that it is the lawful owner of all assets covered by this Bill of Sale and that they are free and clear of any outstanding liens, encumbrances, claims, debts or liabilities due and owing by Seller that could result in a lien or encumbrance upon the property; that Seller has the right to sell said assets to Purchaser free from claims of all creditors or other persons whatsoever, except as specifically disclosed, and, further, agrees to hold Purchaser, its successors, or assigns harmless from any such claims and the costs incurred in defending such claims, including reasonable attorneys fees, to warrant and defend the sale of these assets against all persons and to execute such further assurances of free and clear title to the said property as may be required. *There are no implied warranties of merchantability or of fitness for a particular purpose contained in this Bill of Sale.*

IN WITNESS WHEREOF, the Seller has executed this Bill of Sale this __ day of _____, 20__.

SELLER:

VET FOR SALE, P.C.
By:_____
Title:_____
Date:_____

STATE OF COLORADO }
                   } SS
COUNTY OF   }

SUBSCRIBED AND SWORN to before me this _____ day of _____, 20__, by

_____

                             _____
                             Notary Public
                             My Commission Expires _____
Seal

APPENDIX E

Covenant Not to Compete

COVENANT NOT TO COMPETE

THIS COVENANT is made this ____ day of _____, 20__, between, Vet for Sale, P.C. (hereinafter called "Seller") and John P. Vet (hereinafter called "Purchaser").

RECITALS

WHEREAS, Seller is the sole owner of a veterinary practice located at 2222 Vet Way, Denver, Colorado 80204 (the "Practice"); and

WHEREAS, as a material and separately bargained for part of the Veterinary Practice Purchase Agreement dated _____, 20__, (the "Agreement"), without which Purchaser would be unwilling to purchase; and for separate consideration of $_____ as set forth in Section 1.01(d) of the Agreement, Seller has agreed to the terms and conditions of a Covenant Not to Compete set forth herein;

NOW, THEREFORE, in consideration of the premises, covenants, and mutual obligations contained herein, and in the Agreement, Seller and Purchaser agree as follows:

1. Seller shall not in any manner become interested, directly or indirectly, as an investor, director, manager, agent, employee, partner, stockholder, or otherwise, in any business, or other enterprise that engages in a practice of general veterinary medicine or any veterinary specialty within a seven (7) mile radius of 2222 Vet Way, Denver, Colorado 80204 for a period of five years from the date of closing.

2. Seller additionally agrees not to knowingly and intentionally solicit any clients of the Practice or employees of the Practice in any manner for a period of five years from the date of closing.

3. Seller recognizes that Purchaser would suffer irreparable damage if Seller violates this Covenant. In the event of a breach by Seller of this Covenant, Purchaser shall provide written notice of default to the breaching party by certified mail, return receipt requested. The breaching party shall have ten (10) days from receipt of written notice to cure the default and comply with the terms of this Covenant. In the event the defaulting party fails to cure the default and comply with this Covenant within the ten (10) day period, Purchaser shall have the right to pursue injunctive relief in order to prevent the breaching party's continued breach of this Covenant.

4. If any portion of this Covenant is found to be invalid for any reason, such finding shall not impact the validity of the remainder of the Covenant. To the extent that any portion of this Covenant is found to be unreasonable in any respect, the parties hereby agree to the reformation of this Covenant in accordance with such terms as the court of appropriate jurisdiction shall determine to be reasonable.

5. This Covenant shall bind and inure to the benefit of the parties hereto, their respective heirs, administrators, personal representatives, executors, successors and assigns.

6. Purchaser shall be entitled to seek injunctive relief in a court of competent jurisdiction to obtain injunctive relief and any other remedies that may be available arising from the terms of this Agreement. In the event there is any litigation commenced pursuant to

this Covenant, the prevailing party shall be entitled to collect all reasonable costs of litigation brought under this Covenant from the other party, including but not limited to costs, expenses, and reasonable attorneys' fees.

7. In addition to the other remedies provided to Purchaser under the terms of this Agreement for a breach, Purchaser shall be entitled to recover a liquidated damage amount of $_____ or its damages, whichever is greater.

8. Seller shall abide by the restrictions as to scope, territory, and period of time and that if any court of competent jurisdiction determines that the restrictions of the above Covenant Not to Compete are too broad to be enforced, it is the parties' intent that such court modify the provisions by narrowing the scope to the minimum extent necessary to permit enforcement.

SELLER:

VET FOR SALE, P.C.

By:_____
Title:_____
Date:_____

PURCHASER:

_____
John P. Vet, D.V.M.

Date:_____

APPENDIX F

Promissory Note

PROMISSORY NOTE

$_____.00 Denver, Colorado _____, 20__

FOR VALUE RECEIVED, the undersigned John P. Vet (hereinafter called the "Maker"), _____, hereby agrees to pay to the order of Vet for Sale, P.C. (hereinafter called the "Lender"), at _____, or at such place as may be designated by the Lender, in writing to the Maker, the principal sum of _____ Dollars ($_____) with interest thereon from the date of the Promissory Note at the rate of _____ PERCENT (__.0%) per annum, in monthly installments of_____ ($_____), including interest, beginning _____, 20__, and continuing on the __ day of each month thereafter for a period of _____ (__) months; and a final payment of _____ ($_____) due on _____, 20__. Maker shall pay Lender a late charge of _____ ($__.00) for any payment that is not received by Lender within ten (10) days after the payment is due.

If Maker shall fail to make a payment as required above, Lender shall provide Maker with written notice of the failure to pay and Maker shall have seven (7) days from the date of receipt of the written notice to cure the default. If Maker fails to cure the default within said seven (7) day period, at Lender's option, the payment of all principal and interest due in accordance with the terms of this Promissory Note will be accelerated, and such principal and interest shall be immediately due and payable. If Maker fails to cure a default, the unpaid balance will accrue interest at a default interest rate of _____ percent (__.0%) per annum.

Maker may prepay the principal amount outstanding in this Promissory Note, in whole or in part, any time without penalty. Any partial prepayment shall not postpone the due date of any subsequent payments, relieve Maker's obligations, or change the amount of subsequent payments.

Maker's performance relating to the payment of this Promissory Note is secured by a Continuing Security and Pledge Agreement securing the Practice assets.

Maker shall have the right of deduction and offset. In the event Lender fails or refuses to indemnify and holds Maker harmless under the terms of that certain Veterinary Practice Purchase Agreement, and Maker suffers actual damages that total Five Hundred and No/100 Dollars ($500.00) or more in the aggregate as a result of Lender's failure or refusal to indemnify or hold Maker harmless, Maker shall have the right to deduct and offset any and all damages suffered by Maker against the payments due by Maker pursuant to the terms of this Note.

In the event of a dispute involving this Promissory Note, the prevailing party shall be entitled to recover its costs and reasonable attorneys fees.

Any notice to Maker provided for in this Promissory Note shall be in writing and shall be given and be effective upon (1) delivery to Maker or (2) mailing such Notice First Class, postage prepaid, addressed to Maker at the Maker's address stated above, or to such other address as Maker may designate by notice to the Lender. Any notice to the Lender shall be in writing and shall be given and be effective upon (1) delivery to Lender, or (2) by mailing such notice First Class, postage prepaid, to the Lender at the address stated in the first paragraph of this Promissory Note, or to such other address as Lender may designate by notice to Maker.

MAKER:
JOHN P. VET

By:_____
Title:_____
Date:_____

APPENDIX G

Veterinary Practice Purchase Agreement

VETERINARY PRACTICE PURCHASE AGREEMENT

THIS AGREEMENT is made this ___ day of _____, 20__, between Vet for Sale, P.C., (hereinafter called "Seller") and John P. Vet (hereinafter called "Purchaser");

WHEREAS, Seller is a Colorado corporation that owns and operates a veterinary practice located at _____, Denver, Colorado (the "Practice"); and,

WHEREAS, Purchaser is a veterinarian licensed in the state of Colorado and desires to purchase certain assets (the "Assets") related to the Practice and Seller desires to sell same to Purchaser;

NOW, THEREFORE, in consideration of the premises, the receipt and sufficiency of which is hereby acknowledged, the parties hereto agree as follows:

Article I—Purchase and Sale

1.01. *Purchase and Sale* Seller shall sell and Purchaser shall purchase all of the following Assets:
  (a) *All Furniture, Fixtures, Equipment, and Office and Veterinarian Supplies* and other miscellaneous items used or useful in connection with or relating to Seller's Practice identified herein as Exhibit 1.01(a);
  (b) *Patient Files and Records* All active and inactive patient files and records relating to the Practice;
  (c) *Goodwill* All goodwill, if any, associated with the Practice;
  (d) *Covenant Not To Compete* Seller and Purchaser have agreed to a covenant not to compete which has been separately bargained for and will serve as a contract independent of the conditions stated within this Veterinary Practice Purchase Agreement in the form attached hereto as Exhibit 1.01(d);
  (e) *Premises Lease* All of the Seller's rights and interests in the premises, lease, and leasehold improvements for that certain commercial office space located at the Practice. Seller shall receive credit at Closing for its security deposit, if any, on deposit with the landlord.

Article II—Assets Excluded From Sale

2.01. *Excluded Assets* Nothing in this Agreement shall be construed as giving Purchaser any interest in or to Seller's cash on hand, bank accounts or any other assets not specifically included in this Agreement.

2.02. *Personal Property* All personal items listed in attached Exhibit 2.02 are not being sold under the terms of this Agreement.

2.03. *Accounts Receivable* All accounts receivable of the Practice as of the date of Closing shall be excluded from this sale and shall be retained by Seller.

Article II—Purchase Price

3.01. *Purchase Price* The total purchase price of the Assets being purchased is
_____ ($_____) in United States
currency.

3.02. *Payment of Purchase Price* The purchase price shall be paid by Purchaser as follows:
(a) _____ ($_____) in the form of a cashier's check or
certified funds at Closing.
(b) _____($_____) in a Promissory Note
(the "Note") with Purchaser as Maker, at an annual percentage rate of ___ percent (_%) for a term of ___ (__) years, with _____ (__) equal monthly
installments of _____($_____)
beginning _____, 20__, and continuing on the ____ day of each month
thereafter and a final payment of _____
($_____) due on _____, 20__. The Note will carry no pre-payment
penalty. The Note shall contain a right of offset for the benefit of Purchaser.
The Note shall be in the form attached hereto as Exhibit 3.02(b).
(c) *Allocation of Purchase Price* The allocation of the purchase price is by mutual
agreement pursuant to Exhibit 3.02(c) attached and made part of this Agreement.

3.03. *Security for Promissory Note* The Note shall be secured by the following: (a) Continuing Security and Pledge Agreement and Financing Statement in the forms attached as Exhibit 3.03 covering assets of Purchaser being transferred under the
terms of this Agreement. Said security shall be properly perfected in order to create a first and prior lien on the Assets being transferred pursuant to the terms of
this Agreement. Purchaser shall cooperate in executing any documents and taking
any other action necessary to fulfill the requirements set forth herein, which obligation shall survive Closing.

Article IV—Conditions Precedent

4.01. *Conditions* The consummation of the transaction described herein is expressly
conditioned upon the following:
(a) Seller paying and satisfying all debts of the Practice;
(b) Seller transferring clear title to all of the Practice Assets.

Article V—Assumption of Debt

5.01. Purchaser agrees to assume the following liabilities of Seller:
(a) All telephone yellow page advertising for the period of time that the current re-
gional and metro yellow page books are valid.
(b) Assignment of that certain Lease Agreement for the commercial office space located at _____, Denver, Colorado, subject to indemnification by Purchaser or Seller for obligations arising subsequent to assignment;

5.02. Purchaser does not assume any other obligations of the Practice.

Article VI—Closing

6.01. *Seller Closing Requirements* At Closing, Seller shall deliver to Purchaser:
   (a) Bill of Sale executed by Seller in the form attached hereto as Exhibit 6.01(a) for the Assets;
   (b) All books, records, documents, and contracts of the Practice, more specifically including employee manuals and handbooks; personnel files; training and OSHA documents and manuals; computer data base; computer software manuals; financial records; client handout documents and any and all vaccine and heartworm notification mailing documents.
   (c) Delivery of all active and inactive patient files of the Practice and in the possession of the Seller;
   (d) Covenant Not to Compete executed by Seller in the form attached hereto as Exhibit 1.01(d);
   (e) Sole possession of the Assets;
   (f) Independent Contractor Consulting Agreement in the form attached hereto as Exhibit 6.01(f);
   (g) Any and all other documents required to be delivered by Seller to Purchaser to fulfill the intent of this Agreement.

6.02 *Purchasers Documents and Other Requirements at Closing* At Closing, Purchaser shall deliver to Seller the following documents:
   (a) $_____ in cash or certified funds for purchase of the Assets;
   (b) A Promissory Note in the face amount of $_____in the form attached hereto as Exhibit 3.02(b);
   (c) A Continuing Security and Pledge Agreement and Financing Statement securing the Promissory Note in the form attached hereto as Exhibit 3.03;
   (d) $_____ in cash or certified funds for Independent Contractor Consulting Agreement;
   (e) Any and all other documents required to be delivered by Purchaser to Seller to fulfill the intent of this Agreement.

Article VII—Closing Adjustments

7.01. All necessary adjustments shall be made at Closing to prorate applicable expenses of the Practice between the parties as of the Closing date.

Article VIII—Seller's and Purchaser's Duties during Transition

8.01. *Seller's Transition Assistance* Seller will assist Purchaser in the orderly transition of the Practice in both the business and clinical management of the Practice by acting as an independent contractor consultant. Seller and Purchaser shall enter into an Independent Contractor Consulting Agreement attached hereto as Exhibit 6.01(f) for purposes of outlining the rights and responsibilities of the parties after Closing.

8.02. *Continued Use of Seller's Telephone Number* Purchaser shall have the right to continue using the current telephone number(s) for the current business being purchased. Purchaser shall pay all costs incurred relative to the use of the telephone number.

8.03. *Legal Consulting and Other Fees* Seller and Purchaser are individually responsible for their own legal, consulting, Closing, and any other fees and expenses incurred in this transaction.

8.04. *Sales, Use and Personal Property Taxes* All sales or use taxes due as a result of the consummation of this transaction, if any, shall be paid by Purchaser. Personal property taxes on the assets being transferred in the sale will be allocated on the Closing Statement to Seller and Purchaser based on 20__'s actual personal property taxes and to each of the parties based on their individual period of ownership during 20__. All such taxes imposed by the state or county as a result of this transaction are the responsibility of the Purchaser, and Purchaser shall indemnify, defend and hold harmless Seller and Seller's agents for any liability they may incur as a result of a failure to collect such taxes at Closing or subsequently pay them.

Article IX—Warranties and Representations of Seller

9.01. Seller has good and marketable title to all of the Assets being sold to Purchaser pursuant to the terms of this Agreement. Seller, in accordance with the terms of this Agreement, will transfer and deliver the Assets to Purchaser free and clear of all liens, encumbrances, claims or rights of third parties of whatsoever kind or nature.

9.02. All federal, state, local and other taxes that Seller is required to pay have been paid, and all such taxes which, in the future, Seller will be required to pay will be paid, and that Seller does not have any tax deficiencies proposed or assessed against it, and has not executed any waiver of the Statute of Limitations on assessment or collection of any tax.

9.03. There are no actions, suits or proceedings pending or in process in any court, Board of Veterinary Examiners, or any other organization or body threatened against Seller.

9.04. Seller represents that the Assets being sold are being sold in good working condition at Closing. It is understood and agreed that the Seller makes no other express or implied warranties of any kind or nature whatsoever with respect to the Assets being sold.

9.05. Seller has full power and authority to enter into this Agreement, and this Agreement is a valid Agreement, enforceable against Seller in accordance with its terms.

9.06. Financial information previously supplied by Seller to Purchaser except for ____ expense records are true and accurate. Nothing has occurred in or to the Practice that could result in any materially adverse change in the Practice or its financial condition, Assets, liabilities, or the operation of the Practice. In addition, Seller believes that the majority of Seller's patients and suppliers will continue to do business with Purchaser after Closing in much the same manner in which they have done with Seller prior to Closing.

9.07. The execution and delivery of this Agreement does not, and the consummation of the transactions contemplated hereby will not, violate any provision of any charter, by-law, mortgage, lien, lease, agreement instrument, order, judgment or decree, to which Seller is a party or by which Seller will violate any of the restrictions of any kind or character whatsoever to which Seller is subject.

9.08. Seller is not a party to any written or oral contract for the purchase of materials, supplies, equipment or any other agreement that will survive the date of Closing. There are no undisclosed existing collective bargaining agreements, employment contracts, verbal commitments, or obligations relating to Seller's employees nor any liabilities for accrued sick leave, accrued vacation pay, or other employment agreements, profit sharing plans, or compensation programs covering or affecting employees in any way whatsoever that will continue beyond Closing. Should any such commitments be found to exist subsequent to Closing, Seller agrees to accept complete financial and other responsibility for such commitments and to defend, indemnify, and hold Purchaser harmless from any claims or suits related thereto. Seller agrees to terminate all employees as of the date of Closing. Purchaser has the right, but not the obligation, to immediately rehire the employees.

9.09. Seller hereby agrees to defend, indemnify, and hold harmless Purchaser, any successors and assigns, against any and all damages, including reasonable attorneys' fees, resulting from any breach by Seller of any warranty, representation, term, condition or covenant of this Agreement.

9.10. Seller shall indemnify and hold Purchaser harmless from and against any and all actions, claims, and obligations arising from the conduct of Seller, as well as Seller's conduct of the Practice prior to the Closing, including, but not limited to, claims for professional malpractice.

9.11. There are no liabilities, obligations or claims against Seller of any nature, whether accrued, contingent or otherwise, and whether due or to become due, that would affect Seller's right to sell and transfer the Assets to Purchaser.

9.12. Seller warrants that it has at all times during operation of the Practice maintained in force a policy of professional liability insurance in a commercially reasonable amount.

Article X—Warranties and Representations of the Purchaser

10.01. *Indemnification for Breach of Warranty* Purchaser hereby agrees to defend, indemnify, and hold Seller and any successors and assigns harmless against any and all damages, including reasonable attorneys' fees, resulting from any breach by Purchaser of any warranty, representation, term, condition or covenant of this Agreement.

10.02. *Indemnification for the Actions or Omissions of Purchaser* Purchaser agrees to defend and hold Seller harmless from and against any and all actions and claims arising from the Purchaser's conduct as well as Purchaser's operation of the Practice, from and after Closing, except insofar as the claim arises out of the actions or omissions of the Seller.

10.03. Execution of this Agreement will not violate or breach any agreements, contracts or commitments to which Purchaser is a party.

10.04. Purchaser represents that all medical records of the Practice will be retained for a period of five (5) years from the date of Closing. Purchaser shall make said records available to Seller upon reasonable request at a mutually agreeable time and will make copies available to Seller at Seller's expense.

10.05. Purchaser represents that there are no liabilities, obligations, or claims against Purchaser of any nature, whether accrued, contingent, or otherwise, and whether due or to become due, that would affect Purchaser's obligations under this Agreement.

10.06. Purchaser represents that there are no actions, suits, or proceedings pending or in process in any court, Board of Veterinary Examiners, or any other organization or body that would or could affect Purchaser's obligations under this Agreement.

Article XI - Miscellaneous

11.01. *Severability* If any provisions of this Agreement shall be held to be invalid, illegal, or unenforceable, the validity, legality, and enforceability of the remaining provisions shall not, in any way, be affected or impaired thereby.

11.02. *Entire Agreement* This Agreement and the Exhibits set forth the entire Agreement between the parties. All negotiations relative to the matters contemplated by this Agreement are merged herein, and there are no other understandings or agreements relating to the matters and things herein set forth, other than those incorporated into this Agreement. No provision of this Agreement shall be altered, amended, revoked, or waived, except by an instrument in writing signed by the parties sought to be charged with such amendment, revocation, or waiver. This Agreement shall be binding upon and shall inure to the benefit of the parties thereto and their respective heirs, personal representatives, successors, and assigns.

11.03. *Governing Law* This Agreement and all documents executed and delivered hereunder shall be deemed to be contracts under the laws of the state of Colorado and for all purposes shall be construed in accordance with such laws.

11.04. *Indemnification Procedure* The party that may be entitled to indemnification under this Agreement (an "Indemnified Party") shall give written notice to the party obligated to indemnify it (an "Indemnifying Party") with reasonable promptness upon becoming aware of the claim or other facts upon which a claim for indemnification will be based. The notice shall set forth such information with respect to the claim as is then reasonably available to the Indemnified Party. The Indemnifying Party shall have the right, but not obligation, to assume the investigation and to undertake the defense of any such claim asserted by a third party, including the employment of counsel with payment of all expenses, and the Indemnified Party shall fully cooperate in the investigation and defense without cost to him or her of such claim and make available all records and material requested by the Indemnifying Party. The Indemnified Party shall be entitled but shall not be required to participate in such investigation and defense of such claim and employ separate counsel. The Indemnified Party shall not be liable for any claim compromised or settled without his or her written consent, which shall not be unreasonably withheld. The Indemnifying Party may settle any claim without such written consent of the Indemnified Party, but only if the relief awarded is not enforceable against the Indemnified Party or is monetary damages that are paid in full by the Indemnifying Party. The Indemnifying Party shall satisfy its indemnification obligation promptly upon the determination that such obligation is due. Failure or delay in giving notice of a claim for indemnification and failure to include any specific information with respect to the claim shall not affect the obligation of the Indemnifying Party, except to the extent that such failure or delay shall have adversely affected the ability of the Indemnifying Party to defend, settle, or satisfy the claim or demand.

11.05. *Headings* The headings in this Agreement are for the purpose of reference only and shall not limit, enlarge, or otherwise affect any terms of provisions of this Agreement.

11.06. *Arbitration* Seller and Purchaser agree that in the event a dispute of any kind or nature arises under this Agreement or matters related to this Agreement, the parties shall negotiate in good faith in an effort to resolve the dispute. If the dispute is not resolved following good faith negotiations, the parties shall select a mutually agreeable arbitrator and submit the dispute to such arbitrator for binding arbitration with the American Arbitration Association in Denver, Colorado, within sixty (60) days. In the event the parties are unable to agree upon the arbitrator, the arbitrator shall be appointed in accordance with the rules and procedures of the American Arbitration Association. Arbitration of any disputes under this Agreement shall proceed even though there may be related disputes involving third parties which cannot be arbitrated arising out of transactions involving the parties to this Agreement. The arbitration award may be enforced in any District Court of the state of Colorado or in any court of competent jurisdiction, in accordance with the provisions of the Colorado Uniform Arbitration Act, or any other statute or rule permitting an arbitration award to be enforced. The cost of any arbitration proceedings shall be paid by the non-prevailing party, as determined by the arbitrator, who shall also award reasonable attorneys' fees to the prevailing party.

11.07. *Malpractice Insurance* Seller agrees to keep in force professional liability and malpractice insurance and/or a tail insurance policy to cover any claims arising from acts prior to Closing for any applicable statute of limitations period of time. Each party shall present evidence of insurance upon written request.

11.08. *Survival* All representations and warranties herein made by the Parties to this Agreement will be true and accurate as of Closing, and will survive Closing, and the parties may rely upon the representations and warranties made herein or in documents furnished at Closing pursuant to this Agreement.

11.09. *Notices* All notices required or permitted by this Agreement shall be in writing and shall be given by personal delivery or sent to the address of the party set forth below by certified mail, return receipt requested, postage prepaid or by reputable overnight courier, prepaid receipt acknowledged. Notices shall be deemed received on the earlier date of actual receipt or, in the case of notice by mail or overnight courier, the date of receipt marked on the acknowledgment of the receipt. Rejection or refusal or the inability to deliver because of change of address of which no notice was given shall be deemed to be received as of the date such notice was deposited in the mail or delivered to the courier. Addresses are:

Seller:
Vet for Sale, P.C.

_____

_____

Purchaser:
John P. Vet

_____

_____

11.10. Seller agrees to provide Purchaser with financial statements and expense ledgers for the Practice for 20__ after adjusting to divide expenses between the Practice and Seller's remaining businesses.

11.11. Time is of the essence.

IN WITNESS WHEREOF, the parties have caused this Agreement to be duly executed.

SELLER:

VET FOR SALE, P.C.

By:_____
Title:_____
Date:_____

PURCHASER:

JOHN P. VET

_____
Date:_____

APPENDIX H

Personal and Confidential

_____, 2000

John P. Vet, D.V.M.

> Re: asset sale for practice located at _____
> Denver, Colorado

Dear Dr. Vet:

This is to set forth the principal terms under which Dr. Vet or his assigns (the "Buyer") would acquire the assets of the veterinary practice located at _____, Denver, Colorado (the "Practice"). The sale will be made in accordance with the provisions of a definitive Asset Purchase Agreement and related definitive documents to be prepared and signed by Buyer and the Practice at closing. The principal terms of our agreement, which will be incorporated in the definitive documents to be signed by Buyer and the Practice at closing (the "Definitive Documents"), are as follows:

1. *Purchase of Assets; Purchase Price.*
   (a) Buyer will purchase the assets of the Practice. The assets shall include all furniture, fixtures, equipment, and office and veterinarian supplies, computers and computer software, trademarks and tradenames for use of the Practice name, patient files, and other miscellaneous items used or useful in connection with the Practice (hereinafter the "Assets").
   (b) Buyer will purchase the Assets for a purchase price of $_____, payable as follows: $_____ to be paid at closing; $_____ paid by delivery of a promissory note executed by Buyer, payable over ____ (__) years at an interest rate of ____ (__%) per annum (the "Purchase Note"), with payments of principal and interest beginning thirty (30) days after closing date and continuing on the first day of each month thereafter until paid in full. The Purchase Note shall contain a right of offset for the benefit of Buyer and shall be prepayable without penalty.
   (c) The Purchase Note will be secured by a pledge of the Practice Assets purchased by Buyer pursuant to the terms of a security agreement prepared as part of the Definitive Documents.
   (d) The Asset Purchase Agreement will provide for the transfer of the Practice Assets to Buyer free and clear of all liens, claims, and encumbrances, but subject to the Definitive Documents to be signed by Buyer and Seller at closing. The Definitive Documents shall set forth the parties' agreements as to other terms, including Seller's post-sale services and other relevant information surrounding the sale.

2. *Non-Compete Agreement.* Seller and the principals of Seller shall deliver to Buyer non-compete agreements agreeing not to compete with the Practice for a period of

_____ (__) years in a _____ (__) mile area surrounding the Practice during and after the end of the consulting term referenced in the Definitive Documents.

3. *Consulting Agreement.* Seller and Buyer will enter into an agreement pursuant to which Seller will provide consultation services to the Practice. As compensation for such consulting services, Seller will be paid compensation in the amount of $_____.

4. *Conditions to Closing.* The closing of the transactions contemplated in this letter is expressly conditioned upon the following:
(a) Buyer entering into an assignment of the existing office lease of the Practice upon a modification of terms and conditions satisfactory to Buyer or entering into a new office lease;
(b) Buyer's inspection and approval of all Assets of the Practice;
(c) Seller paying and satisfying all debts on the Assets of the Practice and obtaining releases of all liens on the Assets;
(d) Due Diligence to be performed by Buyer prior to execution of the Definitive Documents;
(e) The parties signing of the Definitive Documents.

5. *Binding Nature of Letter of Intent.* With respect to the matters specifically addressed herein, this letter of intent is intended to constitute a binding agreement of the parties as to the terms to be included in the Definitive Documents with respect to such matters, which the parties hereto acknowledge to be binding and enforceable. This letter of intent constitutes a legally binding and enforceable contract between the parties pertaining to the subject matter of this letter of intent, and statements of intent or understandings in this letter of intent shall be deemed to constitute an offer, acceptance, and legally binding agreement and do create rights and obligations for or on the part of each party to this letter of intent.

6. *Definitive Agreement.* All terms and conditions concerning the purchase and sale transaction between Seller and Buyer shall be stated in a definitive agreement that will be subject to the approval of the parties, acting on advice of counsel. Those terms and conditions will include representations, warranties, covenants, and indemnities that are usual and customary in a transaction of this nature and will require approval of the transaction by Seller's shareholders. Upon execution of Definitive Documents containing the parties' agreement as to the terms addressed herein and such other or different terms as may be mutually agreed by the parties, the Definitive Documents alone shall establish and govern the rights and obligations of the parties, and this letter shall be of no further force or effect.

7. *Allocations.* Seller and Buyer acknowledge and agree to the following allocations, which, are subject to revison by Buyer prior to Closing.
(a) inventory $_____
(b) medical records $_____
(c) goodwill $_____

(d) covenant not to compete $_____
(e) leasehold improvements $_____
(f) machinery and equipment $_____
(g) supplies $_____

8. *No Shop/Confidentiality.* Upon the execution of this Letter of Intent by all parties, the Seller agrees not to solicit, make, discuss or accept any offers to sell or purchase the Assets to any third party for a sixty (60) day period. Seller agrees to promptly inform the Buyer of any offers or solicitations to purchase the Assets, including the terms thereof made by any third party. The terms of the Sale and any information about the Practice shall be kept strictly confidential by the parties and their agents.

9. *Closing.* The Closing of the transactions contemplated in this letter shall take place in Denver, Colorado, at the law offices of Guiducci & Guiducci, P.C. on or about _____, 20__, or as soon thereafter as all conditions to Closing have been satisfied.

10. *Governing Law.* This Letter of Agreement and the Definitive Documents shall be governed by the laws of the state of Colorado.

IN WITNESS WHEREOF, this Letter of Intent shall be effective as a binding agreement among the parties hereto upon being fully executed by the parties indicated below and shall remain in effect as an agreement for the purchase and sale of the Assets upon the terms and conditions provided herein, until superseded by the execution and delivery of the parties of the Definitive Agreements.

Sincerely,

_____

Accepted and agreed to this ___ day of _____, 20__.

JOHN P. VET, D.V.M.

_____

Accepted and agreed to this ___ day of _____, 20__.

Printed and bound by CPI Group (UK) Ltd, Croydon, CR0 4YY

25/04/2025

14662135-0001